# IN THE
# BOOM BOOM ROOM

OTHER PLAYS BY DAVID RABE

THE BASIC TRAINING OF PAVLO HUMMEL

STICKS AND BONES

THE ORPHAN

STREAMERS

GOOSE AND TOM-TOM

HURLYBURLY

# IN THE
# BOOM BOOM ROOM

A PLAY BY

## DAVID RABE

REVISED TO
THE ORIGINAL
TWO ACTS

WITH A NOTE BY THE AUTHOR

## GROVE PRESS INC.

## NEW YORK

FOR THE WOLF AT THE DOOR

AND FOR

LESLIE KAREN OWINGS

*In the Boom Boom Room* was first produced professionally by the New York Shakespeare Festival on November 8, 1973, at the Vivian Beaumont Theatre at Lincoln Center.

Produced by Joseph Papp.

# CONTENTS

Blessings on the hand of women!
Fathers, sons and daughters cry,
And the sacred song is mingled
With the worship in the sky—
Mingles where no tempest darkens,
Rainbows evermore are hurled;
For the hand that rocks the cradle
Is the hand that rules the world.

— William Ross Wallace

The woman is subject to the man on account of
the weakness of her nature, both of mind
and body.

Man is the beginning of the woman and her end,
just as God is the beginning and end of
every creature.

Woman is in subjugation according to the law
of nature, but a slave is not.

Children ought to love their father more than
their mother.

— Thomas Aquinas, *Summa Theologica*

People crazy.

— Sonny Liston

# ACT ONE

# CHARACTERS

CHRISSY

HAROLD

SUSAN

VIKKI

MELISSA

SALLY

ERIC

AL

RALPHIE

GUY

HELEN

MAN

TIME: A little while ago.

PLACE: Philadelphia. The go-go bars, streets, apartments and neighborhoods of Chrissy's life.

The set should be a space with areas and levels similar to a Shakespearean stage, but all within a metaphor of bars and go-go dancing. The bar itself should be most evident at the highest levels; the areas farthest upstage, though deepest in the set, will receive their prominence from their elevation. The farthest point downstage should be the lowest, though there might be dancing pedestals on either side. But basically the downstage area should be least specific of the bar so it can easily become "the street," "the park," "the garden or backyard of Chrissy's parents' home." Mid-level and midstage should be the area of Chrissy's apartment. Perhaps doors on either side might serve as "restrooms" in the bar, yet be at other times the door to Chrissy's apartment on the one hand, and her bathroom door on the other. Though the backdrop for the entire stage should have some element of the go-go bar in it, the set must be capable of allowing the bar element to be reduced at times, and occasionally even eliminated. Mainly the specific "setting" of each scene should be determined by the characters present, their costumes, dialogue, and the very, very carefully selected hand props that they use (which could perhaps be stylized in some way). Once a setting is established, it should be possible for the actor to prowl a larger area of the stage without any sense of confusion about where the action is taking place. There should be a large number of avenues of exit and entrance around the stage and through the backdrop so that characters, when necessary, can appear or disappear from any direction with ease. A bed rolling on from under the upper area might be useful in creating the specifics of Chrissy's apartment: a bed covered in satin, a tawdry color, an emblem and aspect of life in the go-go bar. Or an apron, a mini-thrust stage, might be located midway between the upper level and mid-level, so that it could serve as a place of prominence for dancing, yet be easily used as the bed in Chrissy's apartment. A rug on the floor of her apartment area might be useful, and some drawers built into the front walls of the upper-level elevation might serve as dressers in her apartment scenes. However, there is a danger in too many specifics regarding any one setting in the play. The most essential job of the set is to provide a metaphoric realm in which the specific areas can be made present with great facility, for the transitions from scene to scene must be clear, effortless, and instantaneous if the play is to be most effective. All colors in the set must take their legitimacy from the metaphor of the bar. The lighting must work to provide definition of one area from the other, and time, place and mood, yet always with some relation to the metaphor of the bar.

# OVERTURE

*In the darkness, "Angel Baby" by "Rosie and the Originals"
begins to play. Slowly the soft, dreamy lights rise to show us
**Chrissy**, a young, sexy but not glamorous girl in a rather childlike, or high-school-like, dress swaying to the music. Behind
her stands a man, older, in a dark suit and a tie, a flower in
his lapel. His arms are around her waist; she holds his hands.
Together they sway to the music. Suddenly she starts as if she
doesn't know he's there.*

**Chrissy:** Oh, Christ! Who's there?

**Harold:** Me.

**Chrissy:** Oh.

*(She relaxes, smiles, settles back into his arms, as the instru-
mental section of the music continues. This section can be
looped, or perhaps an instrumental version of the song should
be made with a saxophone lead instead of the vocal. In any
case, the scene now proceeds with instruments only under their
dialogue so that, in a sense, it is their dialogue that is the lyric
to the music. They sway, embrace; dreaming, playful, facing out.)*

**Harold:** Yeh. Now that you're here, got a place of your own,
I bet you think you're gonna get it all done. I bet you think
you're gonna do it all. Sing Rock-and-Roll whenever you want.

13

Play it loud as you want whenever you want. Ruin your ears. Inna middle a the night. Gonna cook roast beef, ham, carrots and peas on a side. Make a salad inna middle a the night if you want. Gonna get boys here. I know. Gonna make love to boys. Sure you are. Blond boys, dark-haired ones, Spanish spics — hot bloods — black boys. Gonna get redheads, ain't you? Feed 'em beef and booze, get 'em in showers — do it on chairs, stools, floors — inna tub. Sure you are. *(Pause.)* See, I'm tired a hiding things. I'm done with concealment. It's a wonderful world an' a wonderful life. I ain't got no health, though I got a little. Whata I care? Let a smile be my umbrella.

**Chrissy:** You come here for a reason, or what? *(She whirls away, spinning in a dance; still they hold hands.)*

**Harold:** Sure.

**Chrissy:** Can I get you a sandwich? I'm gonna have one.

**Harold:** Lemme tell you somethin', though; there's not so much goin' on as you think. Not nearly all that goin' on that you think.

**Chrissy:** You . . . use a key to get in here, Pop?

**Harold:** I'm still around, see.

**Chrissy:** I'm happy to see you. Honest. I miss you.

**Harold:** Don't you forget it.

*(Whenever they move it is rhythmic, to the music. He performs for her, dancing alone. He takes her up; they dance cheek to cheek.)*

14

**Chrissy:** But maybe things are a little different now is all, see.

**Harold:** I'm still here. What kinda sandwich?

**Chrissy:** I'll just keep after some things I can maybe get is sort of all I'm saying. You know.

**Harold:** I'm a permanent fixture. Nothin'll ever take me out. Even when I'm rot an' the rot is dirt, I'll be there thinkin', watchin' everything and talkin' to myself all about it. Sometimes I can even hear the way I'll sound to myself. Real kinda funny. Echo-eeeeee . . .

**Chrissy:** Ham and cheese okay for you, Pop? It's what I'm gonna have. On rye with a speck a mayonnaise.

**Harold:** Tomato, too. Thinly sliced. Very thinly sliced. A little pepper.

**Chrissy:** I've just had some very good things happen to me. I've had some very good things happen to me. Wow.

**Harold:** Happens to all of us. We all do. Comes and goes.

**Chrissy:** I mean, very good things. Very, very good things. Wow!

**Harold:** I been inna hospital.

**Chrissy:** I heard.

**Harold:** Sick.

**Chrissy:** That's what I heard.

15

**Harold:** Trouble in my prick.

**Chrissy:** Oh, yeh.

**Harold:** Yeh. Terrible.

**Chrissy:** I was sorry to hear.

**Harold:** "Penis" they call it. Nurse says, "Lemme see your penis." It's embarrassin', woman like that, good-lookin' woman feelin' around my penis. She ain't enjoyin' it. Nothin' happenin'. Nothin'. Good-lookin' woman.

**Chrissy:** Whatsamatter?

**Harold:** I'm sad, Chrissy. I'm feelin' very sad.

**Chrissy:** No, no.

**Harold:** It makes you think. You think and think.

**Chrissy:** No, no. I mean, what's your sickness?

**Harold:** Infection.

**Chrissy:** Oh.

**Harold:** Onna shell. I never belonged to you, Chrissy. I would throw you up in the air sometimes, you was so tiny, and I would catch you. Up I would throw you, but I never belonged to you, though. You were a joy. I liked you a lot. No bigger than a puppy. "Hello, Hon," I would say, "you're fulla balooney." That's what I would always used to say. How long ago was that? You should come visit. Your momma misses you.

**Chrissy** *(suddenly very angry):* Bullshit. BULLSHIT!

**Harold:** What am I sayin'? I ain't sayin' nothin'.

**Chrissy:** How did you get in here? Did you pick the lock?

**Harold:** It was little Chrissy's father they was lookin' at, I tole them, they hadda let me in.

**Chrissy:** You picked the lock!

**Harold:** No.

**Chrissy** *(scolding him):* Did you break it? You didn't break it!

**Harold:** Wanna go to a ball game? Go see a night ball game?

**Chrissy:** NO!

**Harold:** Phillies.

**Chrissy:** What'd you do to it?

**Harold:** Phillies and Cubs!

**Chrissy:** I don't wanna!

*(Somewhat separated now, they still move to the music as* **Harold** *tries to distract them, to brag and apologize.)*

**Harold:** Me neither! Not really. It's just a lot of worry. It's just a lot of bother. You don't know what's goin' on. So the pitcher's lookin' at the catcher and he's hiding the signals. What's it gonna be? The batter's guessing. But what's he guessing?

17

Then the ball's in the air. Maybe a curve. Will it do what the pitcher wants? Will the bat do what the batter wants? I mean, inanimate objects. Inanimate objects. Who controls these things? Cars run into poles, off roads. What's going to happen? What's going to happen? I'm feelin' . . . so . . . excited . . . I'm feelin' . . . so excited. *(Pause: something is happening to him.)* You remember the way I beat you sometimes with my belt? *(Pause.)* Chrissy? You was little?

**Chrissy:** Huh?

**Harold:** You was little. One time you was crawlin' in the corner, crawlin' to get away. I run after you. Don't you remember I run after you?

**Chrissy:** That was Uncles Billy and Michael, I thought. Uncles Billy and Michael, Pop. Before they went away.

**Harold:** Oh, don't you remember, though, the jolly excitin' way I would sometimes chase you and beat you with a belt? *(It seems he might actually hit her now, so desperate is he to have her remember this "intimacy," these "good times.")*

**Chrissy:** Yeh. Sure.

*(Perhaps he has actually pulled his belt off and pantomimed chasing a child, or perhaps he has pantomimed the belt, pantomimed chasing her.)*

**Harold:** I don't know why I ever did that.

**Chrissy:** Me neither.

**Harold:** I did though, didn't I? See, the trouble in me is infection onna prostate gland's like a shrimp, an' they can cut

18

out the shrimp, but they gotta leave the shell or they'd have to put this tubin' in me — plastic and wires in me. So I keep thinkin' I got this shrimp-shell in me with infection on it, and that's what's wrong with me.

**Chrissy** (*moving to him; they have made up. If the version of "Angel Baby" with the vocal has been used, perhaps the vocal comes back on now. They embrace, they dance.*): You got me all itchy, Pop. You got me all itchy, comin' here like that.

**Harold:** I gotta be goin'. I gotta be on my way. (*Starting to back away, yet holding her hand.*)

**Chrissy:** You got me all itchy.

**Harold** (*having moved to leave, waving from afar*): Hello, Hon. You are fulla balooney. You are fulla balooney.

**Chrissy:** I don't know.

(*They move toward opposite sides of the stage; waving, blowing kisses, moving backwards, almost in slow motion, always to the music.*)

**Harold:** You got a lotta spirit, Chrissy. You got a good heart. Hang in there.

(*Blowing kisses,* **Harold** *backs out and* **Chrissy**, *waving, backs out the opposite side of the stage.*)

\*

*mediately, as **Harold** and **Chrissy** leave, there is loud, harsh, funky rock music, and the lights transform to the harsh, tawdry lights of the go-go bar. **Susan** — sexy, arrogant, glamorous — enters, moving, slinking; she carries a microphone. At the same time **Al** and **Ralphie**, street people, enter, coming in the front door followed first by another man, and then by **Eric** in a suit and tie. **Al** and **Ralphie** carry beer bottles from which they drink. **Eric** has a newspaper. Now **Susan** lifts the microphone, and over the thumping of the music and drenched in the funky cruel light, she speaks.*

**Susan:** And to make your evening at Big Tom's Boom Boom Room more enjoyable, we have music and movies and we have Melissa MacNeil, a Sagittarius, frank, honest and friendly. *(**Melissa**, very sexy, dances on to groans and cries from the men.)* Aside from dancing, Melissa has found that flying small airplanes turns her on. Of flying high, she says, "It's the most rewarding experience of my life." *(Slight pause.)* Ideas and ideas about ideas are abuzz in the brain of this twinkle-eyed miss from the south of Maryland, Sally Hooper. *(**Sally** enters to cries and cheers from the crowd. As she moves near to where **Al** and **Ralphie** stand, she flirts.)* A fun-loving Pisces, Sally loves the Pony, and her many interests zoom from eight-millimeter photography to dramatics to botany, and she can make anything grow. *(In comes a new girl.)* Vikki Bell, however, a Leo, prefers the Jerk. Isn't that right, Vikki?

**Vikki:** Oh yeh.

**Susan:** Vikki goes to college in the daytime where she's majoring in Business Administration, so all you men out there in businessland — wherever that might be — had best prepare for this bundle of more than a little talented determination headed your way. And then we have Chrissy from Manayunk — fresh outa the A&P. *(On comes **Chrissy** in a go-go costume, danc-*

*ing and happy, a good dancer, cute.)* But you better see her quick, because she's just passin' through old Philadelphia like the choo-choo on her way to Fun City. New York-bound.

**Chrissy** *(as she runs up to* **Sally***):* Whooooo! Whooooo! *(She and* **Sally** *switch places as if this is part of a routine; she ends up in front of* **Al** *and* **Ralphie***, who are pretending they can't stand how sexy she is, as if they are going to faint.)*

**Al:** Chrissy, baby, Chrissy, I can buy you a drink.

**Ralphie:** I know the best way. I do, I do.

**Chrissy:** I'm workin'. I'm workin'.

**Al:** We love you.

*(And new music, harsher and louder, stronger in its beat, blasts on.* **Chrissy** *dances; the girls dance.)*

**Susan:** You are gonna like it here! *(Whirling to face the dancing girls, she yells at* **Chrissy***, who is talking to* **Al** *and* **Ralphie***.):* No talking to the customers. No dating the customers. No dancing with the customers. We work twenty minutes on and twenty minutes off.

*(***Chrissy** *dances obediently, trying to do her job, while everyone else departs as if a shift is ending, the bar closing. Dancing, she descends to her apartment area. She stops dancing. If the bed is used, perhaps she pulls it out as one would a hideaway bed, and onto it she flops. The door opens after a moment, slowly, and* **Guy Smith** *peeks in, sticks his head in, steps in.)*

**Guy:** Hi, I'm Guy Smith.

(**Chrissy** *screams, leaps to her feet and runs to her bathroom door,* **Guy** *is following her, trying to explain, apologize, as she reaches through the door, pulls in a robe, puts it on.*)

**Guy:** No, no, no. I live in the apartment just under you here. Exactly below you. I'm an open kind of person with a very active mind—this and that occurring, here and there. I thought I'd stop by. At first I planned some guise—seeking sugar, perhaps, but I found I had plenty, so here I am in complete honesty. I hear you moving from room to room above me as I move from room to room below you—there's intimacy in that. It seemed we should meet. May I come in, I should say. But I am in.

**Chrissy:** You just come bargin' in. I don't like that.

**Guy:** I'm your neighbor. Oh, no, no, I frightened you. Please, no—most important of all—let me set up no erroneous expectations of a fearful nature or of a more hopeful nature—whichever of the two it might be, I don't know, not knowing you—but I can and will promise absolutely that I will make no pass at you, whether you long for it or dread the thought, because I am gay. I haven't always been, but I am now. For the last twelve or fifteen years and I think it's taken.

**Chrissy:** Oh. *(Slight pause.)* Geeze, you just come bargin' in. "Who is he?" I thought. I didn't know you was gay.

**Guy:** Couldn't tell by looking, huh?

**Chrissy:** No. I mean, I knew a gay person in my grade school —I mean a little boy who became a gay person and that was surprising. The other kids would throw rocks at him, and Beinhoffer and Lowell had him tied up out behind the incinerator going to burn the hair off every part of his body until I came out to clap the erasers for Miss Weiderholdt, and I screamed.

**Guy:** So you saved him! How wonderful. Do you work downtown?

**Chrissy:** I'm workin' as a go-go girl.

**Guy:** Oh! A dancer. You know Tommy Berkson? He's a go-go boy — big fat boy, wears net and fringe all as long and lovely as your hair. "It's all molecules and quasars, Tommy," I keep telling him. "All protons and neutrons, Tommy, all doing some very, very celestial Monkey, some natural Pony, some absolutely universal Philly Dog."

**Chrissy** *(pausing to think just a moment, then running to her bed):* See my new costume? *(And she is holding up a white, fur-decorated bunny suit.* **Guy** *is alert, bright-eyed.)*

**Guy:** Oh, it's lovely.

**Chrissy** *(moving, the bunny suit pressed against herself):* Like a Playboy Club bunny suit, see, except I'm makin' fur on it and softer. The real ones are very mean. I don't want no mean one.

**Guy:** What a clever idea! *(He reaches to take the suit from her.)* It's absolutely charming.

**Chrissy:** I know. See, all the girls do it — not makin' bunny suits — some are pirates or Little Bo Peeps. It's what you gotta do to be a go-go girl. Makin' up routines is hard, and costumes outa your head, 'cause then your dancin' is good, 'cause it's

23

outa us. This is the first one I'm makin' a my own. Can't hardly wait till I get it finished. The one I been usin' is borrowed and it's hard it's borrowed.

**Guy** *(having taken the bunny suit, clutching it):* I bet you never have "screamers," do you? You're so vivacious, so open. Terrible evil black moods. I have them all the time: "screamers" I call them. I'm having this affair right now with this lovely boy, but it's doomed. And in addition, I've gotten myself into this perfectly mind-boggling way of making a quick buck so my mood is not exactly constant. He got me into it, actually, Billy did; he's very scientifically oriented. Artificial insemination? Sperm doning? I mean, I don't know how these things keep happening to me! Do you ever have that feeling? There are all these married couples where the husband's straight but sterile, so they inject sperm into her so she can have a child and they have to get the sperm from somewhere so sometimes they get it from Billy. Or me. And I make more in a half an hour than I do in a day's worth of part-time typing. But when Billy's not with me — which is more frequently than I might desire, but he must play the field, it seems — and on those nights I find myself talking to the walls, the floor. May I come to you — feel free to come to you and flop my vibrating atoms down in a chair across from your vibrating atoms and my tongue will vibrate the air between us and you will hear me and think —

*(There is a sudden knocking on the door.)*

**Chrissy:** Oh, my God! *(She jumps to her feet.)* My company. I forgot! A brand-new guy an' I think he's from Bryn Mawr — I mean, he ain't like me from Manayunk. You ever been to Bryn Mawr?

*(The doorbell rings.)*

24

**Chrissy:** Relax, relax. I ain't ready. *(Running to the door, she flings it open.)* What am I gonna do?

*(Eric is there. He steps in briskly, a neat, young man in a suit.)*

**Eric:** Sorry I'm late.

**Chrissy:** You're not.

**Eric:** I'm not? Am I early? Oh, I don't want to be early.

**Guy:** Hello.

*(Seeing Guy, Eric is puzzled. He even steps back toward the door as if he might leave.)*

**Chrissy:** Eric. Guy is my neighbor an' he come up to let me know he lived downstairs.

**Eric:** Oh.

**Guy** *(hurrying to Eric, his hand outstretched to be shaken):* She's intrigued by my idiosyncracies — we have this and that in common. But oh, I'm detaining you, aren't I? From the wonderful evening you're going to spend together. You're a lucky man, Eric. Bye-bye. *(And out the door he goes.)*

**Chrissy:** Bye-bye. *(Shutting the door behind him.)* Wow, he just come in, you know, talkin' away. He's gay, see, which is interesting, don't you think? *(Slight pause.)* I don't know. All the girls at work have friends who are gay and they're fun, they say, and he was so entertaining, like sorta. He's like a girl, but he's not, so you can trust him. Where we goin'? Movie?

25

**Eric:** Movie. Right. Aren't we? I don't want to rush you. I thought you said you thought a movie was a good idea. Unless you changed your mind.

**Chrissy:** No. I wanna. You look very nice in your suit. I think men in suits are most attractive and you have an interesting job, I bet. What's the movie? *(Nervously trying to converse, be social, yet get ready, she steps toward the bathroom door and back, beginning to take the robe off right in front of Eric.)*

**Eric:** We could go to a different one if you wanted.

**Chrissy:** No, no, I wanna, I wanna. I gotta just . . . *(She runs to the bathroom.)*

**Eric:** I mean, it was just one of the most amazing things in my life the way you said "yes," you'd go out with me, even though my horoscope had promised something good to happen. When you simply said, "Sure, gimme a call," I thought, "WOW." What sign are you? In what month were you born?

**Chrissy** *(from off):* My birthday is October 11.

**Eric** *(happily):* You're a Libra. I'm Sagittarius. How long have you been dancing?

**Chrissy:** Go-go? Just a little. *(And she makes her entrance: wearing a sexy wraparound dress and carrying a purse/dance bag.)* I'm ready. Taa-daaa.

**Eric:** Shall we go?

**Chrissy:** Sure.

**Eric** *(starting for the door):* We should hurry, because the paper said the move starts at —

26

**Chrissy:** HEY, BUSTER!

**Eric:** Huh? *(Screeching to a halt.)*

**Chrissy:** You a blindman? I tole you how you locked! I ain't been goin' through this for myself, you know.

**Eric:** Oh, and your dress, too, is very nice. Very nice.

**Chrissy:** Whata people gotta do, punch you in the stomach to make you breathe, Eric?

**Eric:** No, no. *(He is very embarrassed.)* Sometimes it's just hard for me to come out with things like that. It seems phony.

**Chrissy:** Ain't it true?

**Eric:** It's not that it is phony. Oh, no. NO! It just feels that way. Oh, I have a confession. Let me make a confession. I'm in therapy. I mean, it's not really bad and only twice a week, but I'm in it. Not that I'm nasty or cruel or anything. I'm pretty regular, really. I'm just in therapy. Over some things. Not over everything. There must be a million things I'm not in it over. I just have this difficult time living. Though mostly I'm fine. But I am in therapy. Do you want me to leave?

**Chrissy:** Well, Eric, that's too bad and everything, but when you are trying to be with a person who has dances in her head all the time, and who is a special kind of person — I mean, I have dreamed of ballet all my life and other kinds of dancing-so-you-tell-a-story. Of which go-go is just a poor facsimile — and that kind of person must be treated very specially, or they will get upset with you as I just did, and maybe even yell at you. Though they don't mean to, but are merely all stirred up in their thinking. And I thought I should tell you before we went to the movie. And I see you staring at me in such a

27

shocked manner . . . I hope I have not upset you so much you will not enjoy the movie.

**Eric:** Does that mean we can still go to the movie?

**Chrissy:** Sure. C'mon. *(Having taken him by the arm, she heads* Eric *for the door.)* By the way, what is the movie, Eric?

**Eric:** The paper said it started at eight-forty.

*(Lush, elegant, sensual music hits.)*

**Chrissy:** Great!

*(*Eric *and* Chrissy *are about to exit;* Chrissy *freezes and the go-go girls step behind and above her as* Eric *rushes on without her, but as if she's with him. She turns, looks up at the girls, who are lounging, stretching, putting on make-up.)*

**Chrissy:** Hi. *(She runs up to join them.)*

**Melissa:** Hi.

**Sally:** Hi.

**Vikki:** Hi.

**Sally:** Christ, I need another shower already.

*(*Chrissy *is taking off her dress; she wears her go-go costume underneath. She lays the dress down with her purse.)*

**Vikki:** I smell like a skunk; an' I'm all outa Jean Naté. Anybody got any goddamn Jean Naté?

**Chrissy:** I do.

**Melissa:** I mean, you know, Chrissy, if you don't mind my saying so but if you're dancin' and chewin' gum, you gotta learn to keep it under your tongue because maybe it keeps your breath nice, but it looks disgusting.

**Sally:** And I hope you know you shouldn't only be learnin' the down and dirty dances, right?

**Chrissy:** Right.

**Melissa:** Because sometimes it's absolute insanity how bad they want us dancing coquettishly.

**Vikki:** Frivolous.

**Melissa:** Next step Big Apple, huh?

**Chrissy:** That's what I really wanna.

**Melissa:** Anything to get outa fuckin' Philadelphia.

**Sally:** What's Philadelphia ever done to you? Geezus.

**Melissa:** Roy Silk.

**Vikki:** Hurt her a hundred times a day.

**Melissa:** Jennifer got out. An' all her postcards are Vegas and she says the Cheetah Room's a glory, and she says there's go-go in all the big hotels and she knows girls who worked in all the Florida places like Tampa and Lauderdale and they're no better than us, she says.

**Sally:** She was better.

**Vikki:** Remember how she would do "Lovin' Feelin'" for Big Eddie?

**Chrissy:** Who's this?

**Vikki:** Jennifer. This guy'd come in, put down two hundred bucks on the bar and tell her to do "Lovin' Feelin'" just for him.

**Melissa:** Christ, Jennifer could dance to make you cry.

**Vikki:** She did dances inside dances to "Lovin' Feelin'."

**Sally:** Outa reach.

**Melissa:** Outa sight.

**Chrissy:** Wow! Wow! *(Slight pause.)* Whose was that little kid I saw hangin' around here the other night?

**Sally:** Mine! An' he knows all his ABC's, though he's only two and two months.

**Melissa:** You gonna hook on the side, Chrissy?

**Chrissy:** Huh?

**Vikki:** We just like to know who ain't wastin' all their love on love so we can steer 'em business.

**Chrissy** *(as the music builds):* Not me. No. I'd never do that. I'm a dancer. Gonna be a great dancer. Devote all my time to dancin'. Like Jennifer. Get me to be as good as Jennifer.

30

Oh, yeh. Get some Big Eddie — Big Barnie — Big Everybody comin' in here, puttin' down their money. Gonna be so much helpless dancin' tenderness they're just gonna all wanna wrap me up in all their money!

*(All the girls dance, as if practicing, and Chrissy studies each girl, tries to learn a new move from each. Suddenly, the music cuts out and Susan is standing there, having turned off the music.)*

Susan: Sometimes it's interesting to work with no music.

Chrissy: You mean just alone? Oh, no.

Melissa: Yeh. Wow.

Chrissy: Funny moods in my head, they go away in my music.

Susan: Go ahead. Try the Jerk.

*(Chrissy, extremely worried, concentrating, tries several steps, a gesture. She stops.)*

Chrissy: It's hard with no music.

Susan: Try it.

Melissa: See you later.

Chrissy: Bye.

Sally: Bye.

Vikki: Bye.

31

*(The girls all go off, carrying their magazines, make-up, Chrissy's bag and dress. As they leave, Chrissy tries a step.)*

Susan: C'mon. *(She brings Chrissy forward so they are on the apron.)*

Chrissy: I wanna. I wanna. *(And she is trying, arms stretching upward the first move of the Jerk. Susan steps in close to Chrissy, grabbing her uplifted arm, pressing her own palm into Chrissy's stomach.)*

Susan: You don't straighten all the way up when you should. So you reach, stretch. Head back, then collapse.

*(Chrissy tries.)*

Chrissy: Something's not right.

Susan *(stepping away, demonstrating the moves herself)*: It's your stomach, Chrissy — see — the stomach contracts when you come down. You're up. Head back. You come down. Sudden. *(She doubles over.)* Contraction. See. *(And again Susan is tall, stretching upward, and then she doubles over.)* As if you've been hit in the stomach. Intake. Up. You're high. *(And then Susan gestures with her fist into Chrissy's stomach, and Chrissy doubles over, dancing.)* And then you're hit in the stomach. You come down. Arms working against one another. Opposite. You're up. You're high. *(She is lifting Chrissy to stand erect, tall.)* Arrogant. And then you get hit in the stomach. *(Again the gesture into Chrissy's stomach.)* You can't breathe. They like that. You're up. Oh, you're hit. Down. That's good. You're gonna get it. Work on it. Up — hit, down. *(She is backing away.)* Good. Good.

*(Susan goes and Chrissy, alone, practices. After a moment, she steps off the apron onto the floor of the apartment, and sits*

*on the edge. We should have the sense that she is at home;
perhaps she leans back on a pillow, or, after sitting, stands and
practices a step or two. Whatever the case, the door to her
apartment opens behind her and* **Al** *and* **Ralphie** *slip in.)*

**Al:** Hey.

**Ralphie:** Hey.

**Chrissy:** Huh? *(startled)* Hey. How you guys doin'? What's
goin' on, you guys?

**Al:** I bet you thought we'd never show up.

**Ralphie:** We thought we'd come by your place for some milk
and cookies. Ain't you the Salvation Army place?

**Al:** What he means is — we just been in jail till we recently got
out. You don't mind how we come in for a little. *(He and*
**Ralphie** *are already in.)*

**Ralphie:** Day a the week comes I can't do ninety days in jail
standin' on my head, I look for different work.

**Chrissy** *(running to her bathroom door, she reaches in to grab
her dress, as if from off a hook. As she starts putting it on):*
Sure. But I gotta get up early in the morning, see. I got my
dancing lessons.

**Al:** I mean, we been out on that curb for hours, just sittin' in
front a your house waitin' to maybe get a glimpse a you, the
best dancer we ever saw in our lives. You're on your way home
or to the store, we can see you. *(Al, followed by* **Ralphie***,
moves to her to help her on with her dress. They button it:
very provocative, very sexy.)* We think you're the best dancer
we ever saw, the both of us are fallin' in love with you, we

33

wanna come up, tell you. We gotta tell you even though you wouldn't talk to us. We offered to buy you a drink, tole you we loved you right in public.

**Ralphie:** You want me to punch her out, Al? Either I punch her or I punch a wall.

**Al:** Punch a wall, Ralphie.

**Ralphie:** Or that bed. That bed's gettin' ready to jump up and hit me. I'll hit it first. Why'd it wanna hit me?

**Chrissy:** What's he doin'?

**Al:** You should a talked to us, Chrissy.

**Chrissy:** Oh, Al, I talked to you.

**Al:** You said, "I can't talk to you," and run away. That's not talkin'.

**Chrissy:** I gotta sit at the table with the other dancers, see, is why that happened. That's Big Tom's rule. When the dancers ain't dancin', we all gotta sit at the table together, otherwise people might get us mixed up with the hookers. Big Tom don't run no bust-out joint. His dancers are dancers. We got rules.

**Ralphie** *(rushing up to her):* I wanna tell the story a my nickname. You wanna hear the story a my nickname?

**Chrissy:** You a married man, Al?

**Ralphie:** I never had one before. I wanna tell it!

**Al:** Let 'im tell it, you don't mind.

**Ralphie:** I wanna tell my nickname!

**Al:** So tell it.

**Ralphie:** So Al an' me are sittin' out on the curb, drinkin' beer, waitin' for you, so Al turns to me and says, "What's it all about?" You know, meanin' life and stuff. An' it come to me like a sudden excitement in my head—that was my nickname. Al was callin' me by my nickname. "What's-It-All-About." I don't know how he knew it, but he did. So that's what people should call me when they wanna call me by my nickname. I like it. *(Finished, he flops down on the bed.)*

**Chrissy:** Well . . . *(And she pats* **Al**, *flirting a little.)* I . . . gotta be gettin' some sleep now. Maybe you guys could come by again . . . sometime. . . .

**Al:** Ain't she cute? Chrissy, listen, I saw you lookin' at me. I saw it. I'm sittin' down in that bar, you're up dancin', lookin' down, I'm such a beauty.

**Ralphie:** She been lookin' you over for weeks and weeks.

**Chrissy:** No.

**Ralphie:** It's real exhaustin' livin' on the streets, Pussy. We're sleepy, too.

**Chrissy:** Hey, now, I mean, don't you guys be gettin' no funny ideas. You understand me, Ralphie? Don't you be expectin' no dancin' in the street. You either, Al. Don't you be expectin' no heat wave. I just let you come in 'cause how you been in

35

jail — I wanted to talk to you how it was to be in jail — my Uncles Billy and Michael was in jail when they wasn't livin' with us, see — my father, too, even. Did you have any terrible experiences in jail?

**Ralphie:** No.

**Al:** Too many niggers.

**Ralphie:** Yeh. We had terrible experiences with niggers.

**Al:** Which is why that bar where you work is a good bar. No jigaboos, no boons, no spooks, no nigger-lippin' jungle bunnies fat-lippin' the glasses so you gotta deal with 'em. I don't take no shit of 'em, however, ever. It used to be they got their black asses hung or shot, but now they're half the jail's goddamn population. It's got me crazy the way people are doin'. Teachin' that junk right in school. Poor little innocent kids bein' taught niggers are regular people. I mean, everywhere you look there's some white girl on a spook's arm. They're walkin' right up and down the street. That's outa line. That's outa fuckin' line. "You," they're sayin', "Al Royce; you're nothin'." I spit right in front of 'em. I spit right at 'em on a street. I mean, I can see it every now and then, there's a guy and girl, they're different colors, but they hit it off. But what's this current bullshit? This current fuckin' epidemic. What kinda misfit is a person he can't find somebody of his own to be his mate? I mean, I had nuns crammin' that puke down my throat every orphanage I was in — people are this and all the same. All but niggers. And they can have their God who ain't nothin' at all whatsoever, but sure as hell not white, or how come I am livin' in the misery I am livin' in?

(**Ralphie** *starts jumping up and down.*)

**Ralphie:** I gotta go pee. Can anybody tell me which way is the peein' place? Which way should I go?

*(Chrissy points to the bathroom door.)*

**Ralphie:** Thank you, sister, thank you. I can feel my callin' comin'. *(And he is gone, closing the door behind them, leaving Chrissy looking after him as Al comes up behind her.)*

**Al:** Poor ole Ralphie, he can't make you take your eyes off me no matter how he tries. Don't worry. *(His hands on her shoulders, he has turned her to him.)*

**Chrissy** *(looking up at him as his arms close around her)*: What?

**Al:** He won't cramp our style.

**Chrissy:** Oh.

*(Al kisses her.)*

**Al:** He's a good boy. He knows I'm the one you're after. You can get him a blanket an' pillow, he can lay down in the bathtub.

**Chrissy** *(still in the embrace)*: Oh, Al, it was really so pleasin' to me, you talkin' about how you liked my dancin', gettin' me all stirred up in my feelin' and thinkin', 'cause when I was twelve, see, I nearly got run over by a car, see, and ever since that, since brushin' so close with death, dancin' is all I could think about, all a time in my head, all I want.

**Al** *(guiding her backward to lie upon the bed)*: Everybody's gonna die, Chrissy. I been dead myself nearly twice.

37

**Chrissy:** Oh, Al, you got such a sadness in your eyes.

**Al:** No, I don't. *(He presses down upon her, kissing her.* **Ralphie** *comes out of the bathroom and stands looking at them.)*

**Ralphie:** Hey, what's goin' on? She hurtin' you, Al?

*(Struggling,* **Chrissy** *squirms free of* **Al.** *She stands.)*

**Chrissy:** Nothin'. Nothin's goin' on. *(Awkward and embarrassed, she hurries into the bathroom.)*

**Al:** She's gonna get you a blanket and pillow for you, and you can lay down in the bathtub, Ralphie.

**Ralphie:** That'll be real convenient, I wanna freshen up. Take a bath. Sure. I'll be happy yet. Sometimes I think hookers is the only honest women in the world. *(He walks to* **Al,** *who is straightening the sheets and covers on the bed.)*

**Al:** She's no hooker.

**Ralphie:** I can have her when you're done, Al? I'd like seconds when you're done.

**Al:** I dunno, Ralphie. *(He thinks it over a little.)* Maybe.

**Ralphie:** I like seconds. No responsibility.

**Al:** I think maybe, Ralphie, she couldn't deal with it.

**Ralphie:** Yeh? *(**Al** has been doing his best to explain, but it is all very puzzling to* **Ralphie.**) It's all like World War II, huh?

**Al:** What is, Ralphie?

38

**Ralphie:** Life is. Life is all like World War II.

*(The bathroom door opens and* **Chrissy** *comes out carrying a pillow and blanket and sheet, and her dance bag.)*

**Chrissy:** I'm very embarrassed.

**Al:** Hey, all right.

*(***Chrissy*** *thrusts the blanket, sheet and pillow into* **Ralphie's** *hands.)*

**Ralphie:** And "seconds" is the Maginot Line. Dare we cross the Maginot Line? Yes, yes; no, no. *Achtung. Achtung! (Clutching the blanket and pillow, he marches into the bathroom, shutting the door.* **Al** *moves to* **Chrissy** *but she reaches up, stops him, backs a quick step away and starts looking in her bag.)*

**Chrissy:** Oh, Al, listen a minute, Al. I was in the bathroom, lookin', I couldn't find my diaphragm; I couldn't.

**Al:** What?

**Chrissy:** You got somethin'? I was in the bathroom, I couldn't find my diaphragm. You got somethin'?

**Al:** No sweat.

**Chrissy:** No! No, I don't wanna be dangerous. See if Ralphie's got somethin', c'mon.

**Al:** I don't like 'em.

**Chrissy:** Please! *(Turns from him with sudden, ferocious de-*

*termination.)* Please. I can't if you don't. I bet Ralphie's got somethin'.

*(**Al** looks at her, a little perplexed.)*

**Al:** All right. Okay.

**Chrissy:** I was lookin' at you, wasn't I?

*(Out of the bathroom comes **Ralphie**, marching.)*

**Ralphie:** *Achtung, achtung. (He marches over to **Al** to hand **Al** what he needs, and then **Ralphie** marches back into the bathroom.) Achtung, achtung.*

**Chrissy:** What's he doin' all the time?

**Al:** Ralphie's just a very imaginative person. *(He takes her to kiss her.)* You lemme know what you like.

**Chrissy:** I was lookin' at you, wasn't I. **(Al** *and* **Chrissy** *embrace, and far away and above them **Susan** enters almost as if observing them. She has a bottle of wine and a glass.)*

**Susan:** I mean, sometimes I'm just lookin' at 'em all dancin' in some discotheque and all in that candlelight and the musicians and their drums; long, long hair. Robes. It's all just like natives in a jungle dancin' for their god to come like in a goddamn jungle, and when he don't — when he don't appear no matter all their screamin' and all no matter all their yellin', they go off in pairs then, and in despair, they screw.

*(**Al** exits. **Chrissy** turns and stares at **Susan**.)*

**Susan:** And whether he shows up then or not is, at best, chancy.

**Chrissy** *(staring up at* **Susan***):* Wow.

**Susan:** It's just a thought I had.

**Chrissy** *(carrying her dance bag, crossing up toward* **Susan***):* Well, I don't know if I know what it means or not, but it's sorta why I wanted to talk to you. See, I just feel you know a lot about a lot I don't know about. And I admire you a great deal. I admire you a great, great deal, and I was wondering and thought I'd ask what you thought was the appropriate number of times you should go out with a man before you let him go to bed with you. And I was wondering, in addition, if you thought three might be the appropriate number — or four, maybe — whatever, I mean, in order to keep it appropriate.

**Susan:** I don't think there is any number, Chrissy. Geezus. *(She laughs a little.)*

**Chrissy:** No?

**Susan:** No.

**Chrissy:** For none of it?

**Susan:** No.

**Chrissy:** Well, how do you know when to do it, then?

**Susan:** Whenever you wanna. When you feel like doin' it.

**Chrissy:** Ohhh, I need a trip. *(Crossing away to sit on the edge of one of the dance elevations.)* I do. You ever been anywhere? I never been anywhere.

41

**Susan** (*moving to join* **Chrissy**): Chrissy, what if some guy you despise manages to get three or four dates with you? There's no numbers. If you're with a guy, you like him, you want him — set it up. So he's talking, you just look into his eyes real deep, like you're seeing more than his eyes and showing more than your own. In a little, he'll stop talking, he'll kiss you, and if you like it, you just keep it going. (*Giving* **Chrissy** *the glass, she pours her some wine.*)

**Chrissy:** I just think maybe I got a natural talent for keepin' it goin' and I don't ever exactly plan it.

**Susan:** Nobody's very nice to you, are they, Chrissy?

**Chrissy:** Oh, sure. A lot of people. I mean, there was this woman at the A&P where I used to work — I mean, getting back to our earlier topic of conversation — and she said, "You go out with a man, get it over with first thing. Find out," she said.

**Susan:** Well, sure, if that's what you want.

**Chrissy:** But I don't know what I want, see — that's what I'm sayin'.

**Susan:** I mean, it's good to find out if a guy can fuck or not, or if he just goes through the motions. Don't you agree? That's good to do. Nothin's gonna make up for it if he can't fuck. Don't you agree? Chrissy?

**Chrissy:** I just kinda like it all, an' they just all seem to want it so bad. And it don't matter that much to me.

**Susan:** No, no.

42

**Chrissy** (*almost hopefully*): Maybe I'm a nymphomaniac. Sorta.

**Susan:** If it's no good, it's awful, for Christ's sake — you just got me thinkin' back to how it used to be when I let them do whatever they wanted, bangin' away on me, and sometimes I ran into the bathroom afterwards — it wasn't to do what they thought, but because I was physically ill, and I would vomit.

**Chrissy:** Wow.

**Susan:** I just have terrible strong reactions sometimes. It was my wish to be treated as a person. I was a person.

**Chrissy:** Me, too, but, see, I just keep thinkin' what if they didn't want me for anything? I keep seein' 'em all together off doin' everything by themselves, I can't get near 'em, I feel like I'm on the moon. I mean, if they want me for that, at least they want me for something. What if they didn't want me? What else could they want me for?

**Susan:** What about yourself?

**Chrissy:** My what? Oh.

**Susan:** You're a very nice person.

**Chrissy:** Am I?

**Susan:** Don't you know?

**Chrissy:** Uh-uh.

(**Susan** *takes a slug of wine straight from the bottle and paces a few steps away from* **Chrissy**.)

**Susan:** All through my sophomore year in high school, I was in love with a boy and we were sleeping together in the back seat of his car. He was the captain of the football team and I was only a sophomore. Sometimes when my folks weren't home, we would make it on the couch, so one time toward the end of the summer after his senior year, he came by when nobody was home. I could smell beer on him, but I couldn't not do what he wanted. He asked me to take off all my clothes and went to a kitchen cabinet and came back with the butter dish. "I'm gonna cover you with butter, Susan," he said. He moved his hands real slow and soft, butter over every part of me. Then he said, "Bye-bye," and went out the door, and I remember thinking, "What is this to do to the future Homecoming Queen?" and found out the next day how he'd had his first date with a new girl that night. My father had a gun. So I waited in a little park across the street from this boy's house, and when he showed I went over and said to him, "Look what I got." "What?" he said. I waved it. "Wow," he said. "That's right," I told him. And there was this Mickey Spillane book called *Vengeance Is Mine* I had just read, so I said, "Vengeance is mine." "I got a full scholarship for football, Susan," he said. "It's a Big Ten school." And I shot him. I didn't know you could be shot and not die, so I didn't shoot him any more. I just walked away. He lived and went on to play Big Ten football after a year delay. It's somethin', though, how once you shoot a man, they're none of them the same any more, and you know how easy, if you got a gun, they fall down. You wanna go out, get somethin' to eat? I'm gonna go over to Bookbinder's and get myself an elaborate meal.

**Chrissy:** I bet you're a Leo in astrology. When were you born?

**Susan:** July.

**Chrissy:** See? Wow. I'm really getting into astrology. You are a Leo.

**Susan:** Is that something to make you afraid?

**Chrissy:** What?

**Susan:** You're always so frightened.

**Chrissy:** No, nothing. I'm just really getting into astrology. It's very olden and Eric talked about it a lot, so I been looking into it. It's from the universe, and it's neat, 'cause it tells what everybody is and what's gonna happen to you on each and every day of your life, so you can know how to be with people, you can know all about your life. I'm a Libra. I'm gonna figure out my whole life from it.

**Susan:** You know, it's really very hard to talk to you sometimes, Chrissy. *(Firmly,* **Susan** *strides away.)*

**Chrissy:** Don't be mad at me. I mean, sometimes I'm frightened of thunder . . . or lightning . . . or big dogs. *(Trying to answer* **Susan's** *question, she walks off carrying her dance bag to a place way downstage.)* Or, sometimes I'm on the street walking and a car goes by and it's dark and all men in it, and I can hardly hear the car out of which one of them is looking and I don't know why he hates me, but he does, I know, and I shake for fear he'll hurt me in some terrible way, I don't know why.

*(A phone begins to ring, and* **Eric** *runs on above and behind* **Chrissy.** *Grabbing up a phone, he holds it to his ear.)*

**Eric:** Hello! CHRISSY! Fantastic! I'll meet you anywhere.

45

Rome! Paris! Cairo! The park. Fantastic. The park! CHRISSY! *(Without the phone, he runs to where* **Chrissy** *is waiting in the park.)* Listen to me. It was so amazing when you called me, so synchronistic, because I had just that very second finished talking to this woman — this woman *friend*, a friend, a platonic friend — and we were talking and at that instant you called as if you knew what we had been talking about, because I had just figured out at that instant what you want from me. I know at last what you want from me.

**Chrissy:** But I ain't said it yet. I ain't said anything yet.

**Eric:** You don't have to. We had both been raised as Catholics, this woman and me, and I was expressing my memory of a kind of awe I felt toward women as a child; came out of the basic female image of "Mother Church" — and this, I said enabled women to rule men, giving them moral authority, all morality being essentially domestic and thus female in its roots — the needs of the nest, home, family and so on, and —

**Chrissy:** But, Eric —

**Eric:** No, no, wait! Because this woman contradicted me and said that for her, as a young girl, all power had seemed in the hands of men, the priests. And of course she was right. How could I refute her? I couldn't. Until I suddenly remembered, realized — What did men have to give up — what did those priests have to surrender to get power from "Mother Church"? Their balls. Excuse me, but it's true. They had to surrender the use of their balls. And to realize this opened a whole pattern behind me — a way I had behaved, worshiping women, and wanting them, hating these feelings, and on and on I went, trying very gently to find some single button on their secret complicated bodies that would let loose from them the power, the heat, the passion so we would be overwhelmed,

46

overtaken by some natural force let loose from her and neither would be responsible, both innocent. But of course that has never happened. You have to ask. Simply ask.

**Chrissy:** I never been a Catholic, Eric.

**Eric:** I'm asking.

**Chrissy:** I know this, Eric, but—

**Eric:** I'm very bright, you see. Very bright; and so I have a lot of trouble in my therapy with what my doctor calls "false insights," which is where you define and analyze your problem in such a way as to keep yourself from ever understanding it. But this is not a "false insight." It's a real insight. A real one.

**Chrissy:** Sure, Eric. I bet you're right, but—

**Eric:** I have a beautiful room reserved on the top floor of the Sheraton Hotel, Chrissy. It's a beautiful hotel, a beautiful room. We can have it for two days.

**Chrissy:** But, see, the earlier important thing I wanted to be tellin' you is how I didn't oughta see you no more, Eric. That's what I called you to come by so I could tell you. There's this other guy, see, and I'm startin' to think I'm startin' to be wild about him, see. That's what I called you to come meet me so I could tell you.

**Eric:** What?

**Chrissy:** Don't get upset.

**Eric:** What guy?

47

**Chrissy:** There's just this guy and I'm startin' to be crazy about him, you know? That happens, right? And I been in a lotta trouble in the past where I did stuff too soon—too many guys. I don't wanna anymore, maybe, I want some order in my life, I got my new career in dancing.

**Eric:** Didn't you hear what I said?

**Chrissy:** But I got stuff to say, too, Eric. I'm sayin' some stuff, too, ain't I?

**Eric** *(begging now, grabbing at her arm):* We'll talk about it there.

**Chrissy** *(pulling away):* But goin' there is what I don't know if I oughta do it or not.

**Eric:** Don't you like me?

**Chrissy:** Sure I like you, Eric. *(She looks at him as he is gasping a little, rubbing his eyes.)* I mean, whatsamatter with you?

**Eric:** Nothing. I'm just having a little trouble breath—breathing. It's just emotional.

**Chrissy:** Don't look so sad, okay. I mean, I don't wanna be makin' you cry or anything. I just wanna be gettin' some order in my life is all. I mean, okay. But it has just gotta be a deal. I mean, we do it like a "goodbye thing" sorta—just have our fun and go our separate ways. Okay?

**Eric:** Are you saying "Yes"?

**Chrissy:** To a "goodbye thing" don't mean anything, Eric! A "goodbye thing" don't mean anything. Promise.

**Eric:** We'll take a cab. We'll take a cab. *(And he is tugging at her, but she pulls free.)*

**Chrissy:** Wait a minute. *(Moving away, she is rummaging in her dance bag.)* I gotta be sure I got my diaphragm. I gotta be havin' my diaphragm, Eric, or I gotta stop by my house and get it. (**Eric** *peers over her shoulder into the bag.)*

**Eric:** We can do that.

**Chrissy:** No, no. I got it. *(And she lifts the compact-like disc from her purse. He whirls, runs off.)*

**Eric:** TAXI! TAXI!

**Chrissy:** I got it.

**Eric:** TAXI! TO THE SHERATON.

**Chrissy:** Never think about what it's for. All those funny little things bangin' up into it. Lookin' for me. Poor little things. Findin' it.

*(They have rotated now into opposite directions,* **Chrissy** *to the bed where she lies down as if to sleep. To elegant, romantic music,* **Eric** *moves as might a ballet dancer to approach her: yet he is, after all,* **Eric**.)*

**Eric:** You don't know how I think of you. You don't know how I . . . think . . . of . . . all your hooks and buttons. I'll undress you. Take off your coat, your dress, I'll unhook your bra, remove your panties. The room will dim. And I'll make love to you so kindly, so gently you'll hardly notice. *(Here he turns away from her, moves away from her. Another dance.)* And then, in the morning just before mass, in the confessional, I'll

49

kneel beside old Father Kerr, only the wicker confessional wall between us. And I'll whisper of your power. He'll murmer. His burly old head will bow. I'll speak of your sweetness, Chrissy — your fragility. *(He is kneeling.)* And he will tell the prayers of penance that will cleanse me of all the dark cruel longing, the mystery of you. All mystery of you.

**Chrissy** *(to Eric):* I had a lemonade stand . . . at . . . one point in my life. An' . . . I wanted a paper route, but only boys were allowed. . . . We would play "Chase," this game where everybody is on two sides and one side tries to capture all the people from the other side. It was night and I was hiding and I came upon a window. A man was sitting there and he was sideways to me and sitting without no clothes on in the kitchen. A TV, which was portable with an antenna that had white tape on it in two places, was there and there was an army movie on with this actor John Agar playing a wounded soldier. The man in the kitchen was very fat. On the table sat a Cheerios box with one of these magic rings they was always selling for box tops. The ring was golden. Then the man started yelling, "Get out, get out!" And this head of this woman who was his wife was appearing a little into the doorway. "Get out, please, get out," he kept yelling and he never looked away from the TV on which these huge cannons were firing. So I ran so I could escape and not be seen . . . so I didn't see no more. . . .

*(Slowly now the lights have been fading on Eric, who has perhaps turned to look at Chrissy and listen. On the opposite side of the stage, by the bathroom door, other lights have slowly been revealing Al who stands in jeans, his shirt off. Now, as Eric dissolves, disappearing in the dark and exiting, Chrissy turns to Al, fully in the light.)*

**Chrissy** *(continuing; to Al):* The big thing to do was to go over

50

to the stock-car track, and behind the fence the girls who were daring would go to let the boys who wanted to feel 'em up. There was usually ten or so boys and maybe three girls. The guys who weren't feeling us would stand off to the side and drink beer, and sometimes a girl might go stand next to them to listen in, sort of. The cars was goin' round and round behind this big wood fence and this one time this one guy wanted all the way and he was very determined and the other girls told him no, but I thought, "What the hell." You been married, huh?

**Al:** My first wife was a beauty. This was in California. An' I had money. I'd been heistin' gas stations and little stores . . . or I'd steal a car. So I bought a week with a hundred-buck-a-night hooker. I always used to say, "The harder I work, the harder my dick gets," and I was workin' hard. So we got married. She took care of me and I had good soft clothes. I had soft nice clothes all the time and I had money which I could go to Vegas with and lose it if I wanted. But sometimes we'd be out to dinner, there would be this guy who would know her. He'd wink at her. I was like a pane of glass and they none of 'em saw me. I tole her finally how it was makin' me feel real bad even though I was a tough person. "That don't bother you," she tole me. "You're a hard guy. Ain't you a hard guy, Al?" Yes, I was, I said, and went on with that hurtin' in me terrible when she'd go away to work at night. An' I was only eighteen. So I hadda give it up, finally. I wasn't so hard, I was soft in my heart . . . in which I was stabbed by a penknife in my childhood . . . which maybe accounts for something. I was foolin' with this Irish girl and I got caught by her brothers. They beat me till I was beggin', an' then they let me go. Two days later I was back with buddies. We was dukin' everything that moved, includin' this ole man who I was pushin' in a sewer, when this guy run up to me to hit me in the back an' I turned, so he hit me inna chest, an' he had a knife in his hand. I fell right down like I was dead. You ever had a nigger lookin' at you how he wanted to kill you? The other night, I come outa this movie, there was three of 'em leanin' against this wall. I looked once, I knew it cold — if I looked an' met their eyes, they was gonna take me right outa my shoes.

**Chrissy:** What about your second marriage?

**Al:** Very serious. Had a brick house an' a lawn with shrubs, two dogs an' all these goddamn cats. So one day I come home an' I wanted to see if I could get the dogs to kill the cats, so —

*(A car horn honks loudly from off, an engine having come to a halt.)*

**Al:** That must be Ralphie back with the car.

**Chrissy:** So what happened?

**Al** *(heading for the door;* **Ralphie** *comes in):* Hey.

**Ralphie:** Hey.

**Al:** I gotta pee an' get my stuff; it's all packed. We can hit the road.

**Ralphie:** Okay.

*(***Al** *hurries into the bathroom. There is a silence.)*

**Chrissy:** It's so dark.

*(Silence. In the dimness across the room stands* **Ralphie.***)*

**Chrissy:** What kinda car'd you steal?

**Ralphie:** I can talk to you from inside your head, Chrissy.

**Chrissy:** Lemme alone, Ralphie; I don't feel good. *(Lying on the bed, she rolls over.)*

**Ralphie:** You wait. I'll be gone away and you'll hear me. I'll be off somewhere — maybe in the desert — who knows where Al 'n' me'll go? I'll have a piece of your clothing in the desert . . . I'll rub it.

**Chrissy:** You will not.

**Ralphie:** I will. And I'll think things.

**Chrissy:** You will not.

**Ralphie:** Will, too. Right inside your head.

**Chrissy:** What kinda things?

**Ralphie:** Like what I want you to do. When you should go to the post office or for groceries or when you should leave your door unlocked.

**Chrissy:** I won't let you get any a my clothing.

**Ralphie:** How can you stop me? You can't stop me.

**Chrissy:** I can.

**Ralphie** *(knowing she can't):* Cannot. A bra or stocking . . . maybe I already have something packed away.

**Chrissy:** You can't do it even if you have.

**Ralphie:** I can.

**Chrissy:** Cannot.

**Ralphie:** You ever been on acid? It's an explosion. You're born. All light. Like the beginning; when there was Atom, and from the rib of Atom was made Electron, and together they were Atom and Electron and in her center she was riblike, for she was Atom's prickholder in her center . . . a flesh around a hollowed rib. You know that's what you are.

(**Al**, *carrying clothing and an old suitcase, comes out of the bathroom.*)

**Chrissy:** Al, you hear what he's sayin', for cryin' out loud? He's talkin' real funny and scary.

**Al:** He's just foolin' around.

**Ralphie** (*pulling a vial from his pocket*): We have a wish for you to drink this.

**Chrissy:** What? (*Now* **Ralphie** *grabs at her to pinion her on the bed.*)

**Ralphie:** Drink.

**Chrissy:** No.

**Ralphie:** Blessed be the Electron.

**Chrissy:** AL!

**Al** (*more exasperated than concerned*): Ralphie!

54

*(And* **Ralphie** *forces the liquid into her mouth, though she struggles and gags. Then he bounds to his feet.)*

**Ralphie:** Blessed be the prickholder, in the name of the father, forever.

**Chrissy** *(Spitting. It is a red substance smeared on her mouth, her cheek. It stains the floor):* Jesus Christ!

**Al:** Ralphie, we gotta go if we're goin'.

**Ralphie:** That is my blood in you. It curls in your tummy. The holy communion a Ralphie. When I speak, you will hear me inside you. "Yes, What's-it-all-about," you will say. "I will."

**Chrissy:** What did you give me?

**Al:** Catsup, for crissake.

**Ralphie:** My blood. Having taken me in, it will be so much easier for you now to hear my voice, Earthling.

**Al:** I am gonna kick your butt, Ralphie, if you don't stop foolin' around.

**Ralphie** *(whirling to face* **Al***):* I don't have no butt, I'm made of air. I'll have the engine runnin'. *(Grabbing up a suitcase from beside the door, he goes.)*

**Chrissy:** He didn't gimme no blood.

**Al:** No. *(He is finished packing.)*

**Chrissy:** He's a fuckin' creep, though, is what he is, but I could tell right away it wasn't any blood. I don't know why you run

55

around with him. I mean, I'd think you could find a more normal person for your companion onna road, when he's such an abnormal person! *(She has been edging around the bed and nearer the bathroom door, as if trying to decide something.)*

**Al:** 'Cause he's very entertaining, is all. We was on the highway, see, an' I was driving, and he looked at me this once and just outa the blue, he says, "Boy, Al, would you look stupid if I was a cow." I almost drove off the road.

**Chrissy:** I don't think that's funny! *(And with this, she bolts into the bathroom.)*

**Al:** Whata you doin'? I gotta go!

**Chrissy** *(from behind the closed bathroom door):* I wanna show you somethin'. Before you go, I want you should see it. I could have your opinion, okay; be worth your while.

**Al:** Ralphie's waitin', Chrissy.

**Chrissy:** I could give a shit! I want you to see this. You can close your eyes. Be fun. Be fun. *(And the bathroom door opens and she pops out wearing her bunny suit. It is white and soft with a tail, and white fluffy ears. Al stares at her. She hops a little, dances a little, moving across the room.)* I got ears, even.

**Al:** It just gets old when it's with the same woman all the time, Chrissy, an' that's the truth, so I wanna go. It's nothin' personal against you.

**Chrissy:** I could be harder, Al. Whatever you wanted. If I knew what you wanted.

**Al:** It don't work that way.

**Chrissy** *(rushing toward him as he turns and goes out the door, shutting it):* What way does it work? Al, what way does it work? *(She opens the door, yells out.)* My horoscope did not prepare me for my day to end this way, goddamnit. What'd yours say? You probably don't even know. *(And she runs to grab a newspaper, some magazines from her bag.)* You probably don't even — *(And she freezes, staring at the page, reading.)* Oh, God; it says it is a day to do no traveling. It says do no traveling on this day for you will be leaving behind a thing of great value! Al! Your horoscope says do no traveling . . . *(And she runs toward the door.)* on this day!

*(As the door is flung open,* **Guy Smith** *comes in. He wears a robe and slippers, and carries a satchel.)*

**Guy:** Hi. Me.

**Chrissy:** Al!

**Guy:** He's gone. They're gone.

**Chrissy:** Al.

**Guy** *(embracing her):* Don't worry, don't worry. I'm here to make it all better. I'm here with good cheer. I heard all that yelling and banging on the floor — Ralphie with his suitcase — Al dashing down the hall. I knew I'd be needed. I'm so glad I didn't go out of town like I was planning. I mean, I —

**Chrissy:** Guy, listen to me, please — I don't think I wanna be talkin' to you.

**Guy:** You have a screamer coming. It may already be here. Only a clod wouldn't sense it rising in the corners of this room.

**Chrissy:** Honest to God, I think I wanna be alone. Don't make me yell at you.

**Guy:** Go ahead. Feel free.

**Chrissy:** I don't wanna. *(And she flops down on the bed.)*

**Guy:** I have concealed upon my person a surprise for you — an incredible, wonderful screamer-chaser-awayer sur —

**Chrissy:** Shut up! I think I said for you to shut up! Did I not say I am not in the mood? I am not in the mood! I got stuff to do I want it to be alone I do it. I gotta be makin' some resolutions about my stupid life. I can't not bite my fingernails. I can't not do it. I can't keep 'em long and red, because I'm a person and I'm a nervous person, and I diet and diet I might as well eat a barrel a marshmallows. My voice is not sexy or appealing. I try to raise it. I try to lower it. I got a list a good things to say to a man in bed, I say stupid stuff made up outa my head. My hands are too big. My stockings bag all the time. Nothin' keeps me a man I want anyway. I mean, how'm I gonna look like that? *(Seizing a glamour magazine from her bag she thrusts the cover, the face of a beautiful woman, at Guy.)* I can't do it. Not ever.

**Guy:** Me neither.

**Chrissy:** Oh, shut up, Guy. And then maybe I finally get it right and my nails are long and red, I got on a new pretty dress, and I go out — I got earrings and perfume, new shiny shoes and rings all aglittery on my fingers, and they bring me back here and strip me down and a hunk of meat is all I am. Goddamn that rotten stinking Al and let him run off the end a the earth with that weird Ralphie! *(Running across the* *room, she kicks the door; she throws her shoe against the door.)*

**Guy:** No, no don't be angry. No, no. *(Scurrying about to clean up after her, he picks up the shoe. He looks at the shoe.)* Yes, yes, be angry. Be angry. We will both be angry! *(Furiously, he hurls the shoe at the door. He begins to jump up and down as* **Chrissy** *stares at him.)* We will both be angry! Effing truck-driver leather mentality — I never liked him anyway! He was no good for someone like you, Chrissy. A dancer. I could never interest my Billy in the finer nuances, either. Not of clothing or food or even sex. He was so disgustingly straightforward. He's gone from me, too, Chrissy. My Billy. And I'm glad. I spoke to him of evolution — the way we gays are pointing to the future, the way we are the hand of the universe reaching forward in process and evolution. He understood nothing! *(Grabbing magazines, the newspaper, he hurls them wildly down on the floor where they scatter.)*

**Chrissy:** Guy, what're you doin'? You're messin' up my apartment.

**Guy:** We are having a screamer. A fantastic, wonderful screamer. *(He rips the newspaper and joins her on the bed.)* We are going to have stuff all over the place! So many people are gifted with that grand romantic ability of denying all that contradicts their precious hothouse feelings, but you and I cannot deny reality, so we must protect our feelings! I will protect you, and you me. We will be friends. Chrissy and Guy. *(Drawn into his feelings,* **Chrissy** *laughs, touches him.)* All kinds of men will ache to know us, but we will let none of them in!

**Chrissy** *(giggling, throwing newspapers, her other shoe):* I am tryin' to get some goddamn order, we are throwin' everything around!

**Guy:** We will go to movies and twilight clubs, parties. We'll be free. It'll be a joke between us. Aren't you ready for a change?

**Chrissy:** You goddamn betcha!

**Guy:** After my Billy left, I couldn't wait for that goddamn Al to be gone. It'll be you and me. I'll fuck queers. You will fuck straights. And we'll come back here to tell one another of their stupidity — their peculiarity. All affection, all tender feeling will be reserved for us. Close your eyes. Close your eyes. It's time for the surprise. The screamer-chasing-away surprise! *(Having gotten to the floor, he takes off the robe, revealing his pink bunny suit, pink fur, pink tail and ears, but* **Chrissy** *doesn't see. She is sitting with her hands over her eyes.)* It's the way Billy and I were going to go to this costume ball, though it is you, of course, you inspired me to think of it. *(Putting on the ears, he adjusts the costume.)* And now I've had the most wonderful idea! I want you to go with me. I want you to go in his place. Are you ready? Be prepared. Taaaaaa-daaaaaaaa! You may look! *(***Chrissy** *opens her eyes. She sees him. In dismay, she looks at him.)* It's the most exciting idea I've had in my life. Think of it. I'll call you "Christopher." Oh, what a thing you'll be. No one will know what we are. I'll tell them I picked you up at the beach. "I picked Christopher up at the beach," I'll tell them. "He was hitchhiking." We'll be a smash. I know it. What a joke! We can work out routines and dances. There'll be music. Have you worked out any of those routines you were talking about? I've got several down. Like "The Life of a Bunny." *(He does a little bunny dance, a quick little pantomime of hopping, sniffing, a bump and a grind.)*

**Chrissy:** I didn't know you got one, too.

**Guy:** Chrissy, you inspired me! I told you! Some movie mogul will encounter us and make us stars. The misunderstood center of all mystery, we will be stars. And what about the centerfold. Think of the centerfold. Do you know the pose you would use?

**Chrissy:** Oh, sure.

**Guy:** I know the pose I would use. I'd knock their eyes out. Can you imagine if they ever let me? *(In his excitement he jumps back onto the bed, kneeling.)*

**Chrissy:** The pose I would use would be on fur. I've known it for years, the pose I would use. *(To show him, she lies down on the bed facing out.)* It would be this fantastic pose on fur and these pictures all around a me in a bikini on horseback, an' splashin' inna creek, and in the middle me makin' their throats go dry. I got moves to turn any man on. All my life it's been like that, always. *(And turning now to* **Guy**, *her voice softer, intimate, as she rubs against him.)* I . . . just move and they're turnin' on. I . . . don't do nothin', they're turnin' on.

**Guy:** I'm finding it all very aesthetic.

**Chrissy** *(touching his bare leg, their eyes meet):* Whata you think about, Guy, when you think about makin' love to a woman?

*(***Guy*** gets hurriedly to his feet.)*

**Guy:** Chrissy, please, please, don't ruin things. This happens to me all the time—fraudulent women telling me how nice I look, how handsome my clothing is, as if I could be appealing to them, when the simple truth is they cannot bear the sight of a human decent man who prefers men. Chrissy, don't. Just please don't. This is so important to me.

*(Loud pounding at the door.)*

**Chrissy:** Oh, my God, somebody's knockin'.

**Guy:** What?

*(Loud pounding.)*

**Chrissy:** WHATA WE GONNA DO? IT MIGHT BE AL, IT MIGHT BE ERIC! IT MIGHT BE AL COMIN' BACK.

*(Loud, loud pounding.)*

**Chrissy:** WHATA WE GONNA DO? *(She is pushing at* **Guy**.*)*

**Guy:** What? Stop pushing at me. Stop it.

**Chrissy:** You gotta hide. Inna bathroom. Inna closet in the bathroom!

*(Loud pounding.)*

**Guy:** In the closet?! Not the closet!

**Chrissy** *(shoving him off):* Get outa here! IT MIGHT BE AL, GODDAMNIT!

*(Simultaneously, **Harold** comes in, followed by **Helen**. They both wear Philadelphia baseball hats and jackets.)*

**Harold** *(carrying a shopping bag, seeming very worried and* *excited):* I come by to keep you up onna developments a my illness. She wanted to tag along, I didn't think it'd be any harm. Illness movin' right along. Prostate gland movin' right along. Don't you offer me no coffee, no tea. I would die in painful agony before you ever forced me to drink a beer. You could break my arms I would take no whiskey, no water, no gin. Can't pee. You ever been somewhere you hadda pee, you couldn't 'cause there was no place? That's me. Place or no place. I spend my days standing at the toilet. I gotta jump up and down. I gotta sit naked inna bathtub a icy water so cold I can't stand it, then I'm up on my feet, pullin' the plug, fillin' that tub again with hot water an' I gotta sit in it, hopin' my body'll let me pee, waiting to see what it wants to do.

**Helen:** He splashes and sings.

**Harold** *(having flopped down on the hassock, he now leaps up):* I got a rubber duck, got a red mouth, big buggy eyes. I hold his fuckin' head under the water. "Have a drink, Duck," I say. I pull him up: "How you like it, Duck?" He don't know; he's smilin', floatin'. I jam his fuckin' head under the water. It's hard to drown a rubber duck. "Have a drink, Duck," I say.

**Helen:** You got nice curtains.

**Harold:** Saw some a them kids on the street today, Chrissy. I'm so glad you're a workin' person like you do and you're not one a them spacey, spacey people, Chrissy. Them people are scary people. It scares me how they got the whole future belongin' to 'em. I don't know what they're gonna do with it. There was these two of 'em sittin' on this wall with this girl who was wearing slacks and this very short blouse so her belly was showing. Then this car pulls up and this third one gets out and the three of 'em take her into this house. Scary people. You look into their eyes, you see the back a their heads.

63

They look love at you. What's that? That's not a person. It takes you in like fallin' down a well. One of them terrible dreams where you keep punchin' people, but nothin' breaks or holds. Like plastic man. He'd hit you from two blocks away. He'd throw his fist around a corner, hittin' you in the back a the head. It all just takes you in.

**Helen:** He's right, you know.

**Harold:** Is it time we gotta go? *(And he stands up.)* Yes, it is. It's time we gotta go. Goin' to the ball game. It's Bat Day. Last week was Helmet Day. *(And he pulls out a baseball batter's helmet from the shopping bag. He puts it on.)* An' I got a Phillies fan button. You wanna go? In another week I'll be a fully outfitted player. C'mon! *(He heads for the door.)*

**Chrissy:** Can't.

**Helen:** I knew she wouldn't.

**Harold** *(leaving):* Well, I am and I don't wanna be late no more.

**Helen** *(stopping by the door):* I thought I noticed certain articles of clothing lying around that are usually worn by men.

**Chrissy:** You're very observant.

**Helen:** That's what I thought.

*(**Helen** goes, and **Guy** steps out from the opposite side of the stage.)*

**Guy:** I'm going to be calm about this, Chrissy, but I am not going to bury my feelings, when you have committed this

64

cruelty . . . or if that's too strong—at least this thoughtless indiscretion—*(He has run to the dance bag he carried in at his entrance)* at the very outset, the so-to-speak "christening" of our new relationship, treating me shamefully.

**Chrissy:** Guy, I am not feeling well at this moment. Please, please don't be yellin' at me.

**Guy:** No, no, no. Aren't you listening? *(As he approaches her with a make-up brush, compacts, vials, taken from the bag.)* I'm going to put this on you.

**Chrissy:** What?

**Guy:** I want us to have fun. We were having so much fun.

**Chrissy:** What is it?

**Guy:** Glitter. For the party. *(He starts applying the glitter.)* Everyone will have it. I want us to be spectacular. "Christopher and I met," I will say, "in New York. In a bar. *Boot Hill.*" All the people at the party are in one form of show biz or another; several ballet dancers, and they'll be wearing glitter. I want us to—

**Chrissy** *(pulling away):* I ain't no "Christopher," Guy. I don't wanna go nowhere as no "Christopher." I am a "Chrissy." I don't wanna do this.

**Guy:** But we made a plan.

**Chrissy:** No. I don't feel so good, see. *(She rolls away on the bed, turning her back on him, curling up.)*

**Guy:** I feel awful. Is that the point? I mean, I am personally

65

in despair. La la. (*And he starts making himself up as he sits there, looking into the mirror in the compact, putting on glitter, eye shadow.*) But isn't that the *sine qua non* of our time, that out of our absurdity, we must create — must we not — by our wit and cunning, the delight of our survival? If our lives are a joke of such perfection as to be a triumph of ridiculousness, then I say, "Enjoy the joke!" I mean, after all, I'm an artificial inseminator! I'm a sperm donator! (*More or less finished with himself now, he moves to her, trying to get her to sit up so he can put glitter on her.*) I have these goddamn doctors who used to tell me it would ruin my brain now paying me good money to go to this white antiseptic room and jerk off in a bottle, while the couple it's for sit off somewhere and hold hands and plan families and everybody pretends their union isn't simply and truly as barren as all of mine. Ohhh, if just once they would be informed that the thing getting fat in the little woman's tumtum is the seed of a gay. Wouldn't that have them purely paranoid over little lollykins going to be under their Christmas tree for the next twenty years? I mean, I used to worry that being gay I'd never have any children but pretty soon, thanks to Science, I'll have forty or fifty running loose, which I'll never see. But then someday, of course, they'll have incubators, and some man and me can fertilize an egg and have it right there to raise; first his, then mine. C'mon, let me put this on you. (*As he tugs at her she looks up, rolls away, sitting up. He stares at her.*) Ohhh, honey, you're crying. Don't cry. (*Hurrying to her, he puts his arm around her.*)

**Chrissy:** Oh, God, I am tired. Would you understand how it is depressing for me to have moved from one neighborhood to another four hundred and fifty times, looking for a man, and ended up with a faggot inna bunny suit.

**Guy:** Now, please, Chrissy, we're having fun.

**Chrissy:** Well, it's the truth, ain't it? I mean, you are a god-damn faggot can't go near a woman but he's gotta be in one room and her in another, walls between 'em.

**Guy:** Now, Chrissy, calm down; calm down. I'll tell you some tricks to do to a man in bed that drive him wild.

**Chrissy:** That's disgusting, Guy! What are you talkin' about?

**Guy:** I'm only trying to be helpful—speaking only out of good-heartedness! I mean, it must have occurred to you that perhaps the reason no man is here with you is because you don't quite know how to be good for any of them.

**Chrissy:** I'm plenty good for 'em. Better'n you, that's for sure.

**Guy:** You're not just born with the right to them, you know.

**Chrissy:** Goddamnit, Guy.

**Guy:** You've got to do more than just lay there!

**Chrissy:** Shut up!

**Guy:** You've got to stop being so spoiled and childish. There are ironies we must accept in tolerance and good humor. I could change their lives. Oh, yes, they wander up the stairs passing my door and on to you. But I don't stop them—I let them go—knowing all the while that given half an hour with any one of them, you'd never see them again.

**Chrissy:** Bullshit.

**Guy:** And the irony beyond endurance is that I'm a better dancer than you.

**Chrissy:** Bullshit, Buster Brown!

**Guy:** Stop yelling at me, you dizzy cunt!

**Chrissy:** I don't wanna be standin' in no room yellin' at no faggot! I don't wanna be standin' in no room yellin' at no—

**Guy:** How can you insult me? You can't insult me. My mind is fire and you plod all around me! We who are the experiment are more in need of explanation than you who endlessly repeat the failed universe!

**Chrissy:** Gimme that bunny suit.

**Guy:** What?

**Chrissy:** Get outa that bunny suit before I rip it off you! *(Struggling with him, she pulls the tail off, bends the ears.)*

**Guy:** Oh, you want me to get all excited, don't you? Start yelling and calling names, but I am not an excited person. I'll wear this bunny suit if I want! I MADE IT!

**Chrissy:** But I thought it up a my own idea. You got no right to it, no right to any of it, bein' so graceful all the time, so elegant and neat.

**Guy:** Oh, what kind of a career will you have you can't even outdance a man.

**Chrissy:** GET OUTA THAT BUNNY SUIT, GODDAMNIT!

**Guy:** It's mine!

**Chrissy:** It's mine! *(Frantically, she is tearing at her bed.)*

**Guy:** It's mine!

**Chrissy** (*rising up, she has pulled out a huge scissors from a hiding place in the bed*): I'LL CUT YOUR FUCKIN' HEART OUT! (*She runs at him, the scissors raised, and he flees backward. She falters, looks at the scissors in her hand. Her hand trembles.* **Guy** *stares at her.*) Whatsa matter with me?

**Guy:** Oh, look at you — you could be a centerfold just as you are: perfect *Playboy* centerfold — with a cleaver in your hand! (*And turning, he heads for the door.*)

**Chrissy:** Get outa here, you faggot. (*She drops the scissors as he exits.*) Fuckin' faggot. I'd be a good one. I would. What's a faggot know? What's a faggot know about a woman? (*And she begins to pace now, music rising.*) I mean, Sally's such a clever girl, her hair always long and clean. I can do like Sally — get my hair longer, cleaner. They like that. (*She is pacing, the music building.*) And I can be more careful about having no hair on my arms or under my arms, like Vikki. I got too much hair on my arms and under my arms. I'll buy all new lingerie. Or maybe I shouldn't wear a bra. I should stop wearing a bra. (*And she has stopped; the music plays.*) I'd be a good one. I'd be the best one, sittin' in fur, and they'd polish me, make me smooth and glossy — all my marks away. Airbrush me till I'd gleam. You gotta like bein' a woman. You gotta accept all aspects of your body — breasts — reproductive organs . . . You're high. Arrogant. And then you're hit. Oh! You're up. You're hit. Oh! . . . I'm gonna be on horseback inna bikini! I'm gonna be sittin' in fur, this mink curlin' down, and they polish me till I gleam, and I'm golden. I'm gonna be golden. I wanna be golden. I gotta be golden. (*She stands, posing in the light as the music and lights fade to dark and silence.*)

**END OF ACT ONE**

# ACT TWO

TIME: The same.

PLACE: The same.

(*Music. Lights. Big Tom's bar. The girls,* **Vikki, Melissa, Sally** *and* **Chrissy** *all dance, and then* **Susan** *enters, carrying her mike.*)

**Susan:** Gotta take a minute to do a promo for the owner of this place — Big Tom — he'd do it himself, but he's so shy. He's here, though. You might see him. He's not unfriendly, just busy. (*Then calling off.*) You here, Tom? Give a yell. (*Then back to the audience.*) Sometimes he's around the corner — you know the place I mean — the Room Tomasita, where men dance only for men — and then he's gotta spend some time right upstairs in the Tom-Tom Room, where women dance only women. He's gotta make his rounds, 'cause he owns them all. He wanders all three like a man through a single home, making sure the jukebox songs are current, the customers grinning, the hookers polite and busy. It's a giggle to him — the way those girls can do such a job on a john, but they gotta read "Dear Abby" to understand their lives. Watch for a hooker to take off her shoes as she stands at the bar workin' her trade. Then look for a bright-eyed man strolling the aisles, and suddenly he stops to nudge the hooker's shoe back under the bar with a wink. That's Tom. Say "Hello."

(*Now the music is a little louder.*)

**Susan:** Sometimes he sends out a girl to Pony to applause in a boy's gay bar. *(Looking at* **Chrissy,** **Susan** *gestures for* **Chrissy** *to go, and after a "Who me?" look from* **Chrissy,** *she goes off.)* Or a boy comes here to do his best for a song. *(On comes a boy in a leather costume: hat, sunglasses, jeans and leather jacket, to dance in the spot* **Chrissy** *just left.)* Tom likes his family friendly. He likes his house neat. *(And* **Susan** *now stops, walks over to the side for a drink as the girls dance.)* Isn't Vikki doing the Pony a lovely sight? Don't you think of a plain upon which she prances, nature's girl, until she joins Melissa doing the Monkey; the downbeat slamming the knees and the hands are a monkey's climbing high upon an imaginary vine, where you are hit in the stomach and fall, like Sally, into the Jerk.

*(Now the music is loud and the other girls dance while* **Chrissy** *enters, wearing a simple, slightly childlike dress and carrying a thermos of coffee; she walks to* **Susan,** *and pours her a cup of coffee. As the other girls leave one by one, the music fading,* **Susan** *sits and* **Chrissy** *begins rubbing the back of* **Susan's** *neck. Then everyone is gone but* **Susan** *and* **Chrissy,** *the music changed to a different tune and very soft, as if a radio is playing nearby.)*

**Chrissy:** You never been interested in astrology, huh?

**Susan:** No, why?

**Chrissy:** It's got a long history; Greeks even. You like the coffee I made you?

**Susan:** Sure.

**Chrissy:** Wasn't that amazin', somebody spittin' in Melissa's shoe? And do you know what? I'm the one who spit in it!

74

**Susan:** You spit in her shoe?

**Chrissy** *(moving away):* Oh, she's so good. You know she is. I'll never be that good. It's because she's ballin' that nigger.

**Susan:** Maybe you should tell her that's why she's so good; she could quit practicin'.

**Chrissy:** I don't know. Maybe. I mean, like I been doin' a number a funny things lately. See, I was in New York last week 'cause I just wanted to be and get outa stupid Philadelphia, so I got in this bar and was picked up by this funny little soldier in this soldier suit. He kept talkin' how he hadda go to this foreign country — I never heard of it — where there was, he said, danger, and he was very afraid though he was actin' other. So when he got me back to the hotel, he kissed me. I put my tongue real deep into his mouth, till I felt him turn on. Then I left him standin' there and I felt real pleased how I was leavin' him. But now I'm ashamed. I mean, whatsamatter with me? We got no right to be bad to men. Nothin' ever works out for them. They just try and try.

**Susan:** You know what you're sayin' about men most of the time is a buncha crap.

**Chrissy:** And I went to one a them topless dancin' places in New York, you know? You ever work in one a them places?

**Susan:** What? Topless? Not on your life.

**Chrissy:** Me neither, I wouldn't either, ever. *(She crosses back to* **Susan**.) There was this really beautiful girl I saw I couldn't believe the stuff she was doin'. I mean, rubbin' herself between her legs and pretendin' to lick her fingers then. That's dis-

gustin'. And all the girls doin' different stuff; and not together or to the music even, the men all just lookin' at 'em. And
she coulda been a great dancer, too — this one girl. I could see
she coulda, but she was just doin' this shit. And she was so
pretty. What was she doin'? Dancin's gotta have prettiness
in it.

**Susan** (*sipping the coffee*): You shoulda spit in her shoe.

**Chrissy:** Yeh. She didn't have any shoe. You want more coffee? I got more.

**Susan** (*pushing the coffee away*): No.

**Chrissy:** See, I just gotta tell you somethin'. (*Rising abrupt-
ly, she begins to pace.*) See, I just been more nervous than I
think I oughta from the time Al left. So I been figurin' there's
somethin' wrong with me in my mind maybe the way I always
got no luck and I oughta get it straightened out so I can get
on with my career in my dancin' and have some luck. See, and
Eric was talkin' always about this underplace is in us from his
therapy. So I been thinkin' maybe the way my Uncles Billy
and Michael beat me sometimes is down there — or my father
with a belt, he says, but I don't remember it — but that's all
just wounds of the body is my point, and they heal unlike those
of the spirit which is where the underplace is, I would guess.
You know about this?

**Susan:** Some.

**Chrissy:** Ain't it somethin'? This stuff down there talkin' to us
about what we should do, we think it's us, but it's it — we don't
know what we're doin'. So I been thinkin' and thinkin' and
maybe the bad stuff done to me is the way my momma made
me nearly a abortion.

76

**Susan:** What?

**Chrissy:** See, my momma didn't wanna have me as a baby.

**Susan:** Whaddaya mean?

**Chrissy:** It's true, I know it is.

**Susan:** You couldn't possibly know that.

**Chrissy:** She tole me. She had two others before I was even there, and then she tried one on me but it didn't work.

**Susan:** She told you she didn't wanna have you?

**Chrissy:** One afternoon. We were very poor. We were very, very poor. So I'm thinkin' about mental therapy, Susan. You think I should or I shouldn't?

**Susan:** You thinkin' about individual or group? It can be good sometimes, as long as you go to a woman's group or an individual woman therapist; but go to a woman.

**Chrissy:** Oh, I couldn't do that.

**Susan:** It's best, believe me. I was with this woman's group for six months or so and I found out a lot. Or all I needed. After just a little I was able to say what I needed. You go to a man therapist, you'll get the meaning of the word — "ther-a-pist." The Rapist. *(And she laughs a little.)* Yeh, I was doin' this crossword puzzle — all of a sudden, I saw — that's what it was. The Rapist. Exactly what he'll do to your mind. I'm so much freer now, Chrissy, believe me.

**Chrissy:** That's what I want. I'm very sensitive to everything.

77

I mean, inside right now, I don't believe you really think my coffee I made is good, you're just sayin' it. I mean, whata you think a me, Susan? Like if you was to point me out on the street and describe me to somebody who don't know me at all, what would you say?

Susan: Well, I—Whata you mean?

Chrissy (*leaping to her feet*): See! See! I could do it about you in a second. It would be so damn easy about you. You're so proud and capable. Leo's are exactly what you are. But I'm a Libra—my sign is scales and balance. I'm supposed to be dedicated to justice and harmony. I'm supposed to be a born mediator—I don't even know what's goin' on, for crissake. And on the other I'm whimsical an' moody an' sentimental. I got all the bad and none a the good, or maybe I got none a them. Would you say I got some? It's so depressin'.

Susan: You have a lovely gentleness about you, Chrissy.

Chrissy: Think a what I did to that poor soldier and he was so scared.

Susan: He was a jerk.

Chrissy: He just didn't know the rules. I'm speaking out for fairness like I gotta if I'm ever gonna be a Libra! (**Chrissy** *flops down beside* **Susan**. **Susan** *sits quietly, looking at* **Chrissy**.)

Susan: It's their pride, Chrissy; their goddamn pride. Each and every man in the world thinkin' he's got some special inner charm we all of us just been waitin' to have.

Chrissy: They don't mean to hurt us.

**Susan:** Chrissy, is that what you believe?

**Chrissy:** It's true. I know it is. They just don't know how not to.

*(And there is a silence as* **Susan** *reaches across the table to touch* **Chrissy**.*)*

**Susan:** I want to make love to you, Chrissy.

**Chrissy:** Huh?

**Susan:** Didn't you hear me?

**Chrissy:** Huh?

**Susan:** Have you ever made love with a woman?

**Chrissy:** I'm gonna get a drink of water. *(She starts to rise, but* **Susan** *holds on.)*

**Susan:** They prize themselves so highly, sitting out there when we're dancing, thinking it's them making us move so fancy — and the fancier we move, the better they think they are. So they give gifts for special dances and then think they're the ones making you move in that beautiful way they know they could never make you move in bed. I take no gifts. They like to think of themselves as weapons entering flesh — making life or death. I think of them as a straw going into the sea and the sea, scarcely noticing, takes them in. I turn on their feeble minds from as far away as the moon.

**Chrissy:** Don't you like them? I thought you did.

79

**Susan:** I did. I do. I will again. But there are so many ways of making do.

**Chrissy:** But I . . . want a relationship.

**Susan:** I could give you that.

**Chrissy:** But you're not a man, see?

**Susan:** No.

**Chrissy:** See?

**Susan:** I'm a person.

**Chrissy:** But what would I be? I don't know.

**Susan:** You would be a person, too; we would be two people.

**Chrissy:** But would I be a man person or a woman person?

**Susan:** You would be yourself.

**Chrissy:** But that's what I don't know what it is. I don't.

**Susan:** You make too much of it.

*(With **Susan's** line, a man, a janitor, enters with a broom, as if it is the bar late at night; he starts to sweep up. His presence, of course, settles the issue for **Chrissy**.)*

**Chrissy:** I wanted you to help me, tell me, Susan!

**Susan:** You've got to stop being afraid of everything!

**Chrissy:** I have! I stare down people on the subways all the time now. I don't care what they are or how big they are; I stare 'em down.

**Susan** (*gathering up her things, some books, her purse*): I'm going. Got classes tomorrow.

**Chrissy:** I didn't wanna make you feel bad.

(**Susan** *stops. She looks at* **Chrissy**.)

**Susan:** Chrissy, it's really very nice. It's like you do it to yourself, only it's a surprise.

**Chrissy:** Oh.

**Susan:** Yes.

**Chrissy:** Thank you for asking. And don't be mad at me, okay.

**Susan:** No.

(*Noise, laughter, music as* **Sally, Melissa, Vikki** *enter from the opposite side of the stage. They are dressed in street clothes and carry a radio playing a pop tune. The girls yell to* **Susan,** *"C'mon, Susan. Let's go." They ad-lib a line or two about what and where they want to go to eat. The janitor exits now; if chairs have been used for the scene with* **Susan** *and* **Chrissy,** *he takes the chairs with him as he leaves.*)

**Susan:** I'll see you at work.

(**Susan** *hurries to join the girls, as* **Chrissy** *trails along, watching and waving as they depart, while behind her at the lower* *opposite corner,* **Harold** *has entered in the dark to sit, sharpening his sickle. The music fades to silence in which there is heard the grinding of the sickle on the whetstone.)*

**Chrissy** *(turning to look at* **Harold***):* Hi, Pop.

**Harold:** Sharpening a sickle. Gonna sharpen the sickle, and then the mower; after that the hoe, the spade and the rake.

**Chrissy** *(hurrying to sit down beside him):* Want a sip of my coffee? I've got it here — right here in my thermos; I've started carrying a thermos bottle of coffee around where I go, and offering it to people.

**Harold:** Don't mind if I do.

**Chrissy** *(busily getting him the coffee):* It makes me feel that people like me. I work very hard at making the coffee good. The only problem is there's four ways to make it — I mean, black, or with sugar, or with cream, or with cream and sugar. I couldn't figure it for a little and so I thought of maybe switching to some other beverage and then I just decided the hell with it, I'd use cream only, and the black-and-sugar people would probably be able to drink it without a lot of trouble. Only those who like it black would be left out.

**Harold:** You could carry sugar separate.

**Chrissy:** What?

**Harold:** You could carry sugar and cream separate.

**Chrissy** *(the idea making her very happy):* Sure!

**Harold:** You could have them in little packets.

**Chrissy** *(even happier):* That's a good idea.

**Harold** *(standing with his sickle):* I'm going to take the sickle and clean out a patch a ground in my garden place out beside the garage. There's a lot of weeds there. I'll cut them down. Then I'll use the mower and then the hoe and shovel to break up the ground. I'm going to plant some flowers. I'll use the hoe to keep out the weeds. Weeds'll come to choke the flowers. I'll use the hoe to kill the weeds.

**Chrissy:** I'm thinking about going into therapy. I thought I would mention it to you. You know what mental therapy is?

**Harold** *(sitting back down):* Ain't no secrets inna world no more, Chrissy.

**Chrissy:** I'm thinking about it. I'm thinking maybe I need it.

**Harold:** I had a little some of that second time I was in jail.

**Chrissy:** I didn't know that.

**Harold:** Didn't like it. Ask you a lot of questions about yourself. Personal questions. None of their business. *(He is very emphatic about this.)*

**Chrissy:** They're supposed to, I think.

**Harold:** Didn't like it.

**Chrissy:** That's how it works, I think.

**Harold:** Some people like it.

83

**Chrissy:** Well, I'm thinking about going into it. I'm having a lot of troubles. I cry a lot.

**Harold:** Life's sad, Chrissy; makes you cry.

**Chrissy:** No, no, I mean, for no reason.

**Harold:** It's all in your mind.

**Chrissy:** That's what I'm saying. I don't know the reasons.

**Harold:** It'll go away. That's all I know. It'll go away and then it'll come back. And then it'll go away. Problem's only trouble is you worry about it.

**Chrissy:** I'm worried, see, that's what I'm saying.

**Harold:** No point.

**Chrissy:** You remember when I was a baby and you gimme all that vodka. You gimme all that vodka in my baby bottle.

**Harold:** You don't remember that. Don't tell me you remember that.

**Chrissy:** No, no, I was a baby. I heard. Uncle Billy and his girlfriend bet their baby could outdrink me. You hadda contest.

**Harold** (*very disappointed*): Wasn't much of a contest, lemme say. No contest whatsoever.

**Chrissy:** Didn't you know it would hurt me?

**Harold** (*very, very disappointed*): Their baby was older, and he threw up and you went to sleep. That's no contest. We'd been drinkin' and listenin' to baseball on the radio. It was World Series on the radio. Yankees won it.

**Chrissy:** But didn't you know it would hurt me?

**Harold:** It didn't hurt you bad, Chrissy!

**Chrissy:** I hadda go inna hospital.

**Harold:** I just got outa jail on parole and we was celebratin', Chrissy, that's what happened. Your momma said it wouldn't hurt you bad.

**Chrissy:** 'Cause she wanted me dead, which is the way she always wanted me like I was somethin' that oughta be dead. I don't oughta be dead. Leave her.

**Harold:** I been in jail too many times.

**Chrissy:** She never wanted me; you wanted me.

**Harold:** Every time I leave her, see, I end up in jail.

**Chrissy:** She got no right to have you. She wanted me dead.

**Harold:** I dunno.

**Chrissy:** She got no feelin' for anybody but herself. She's a dirty filthy woman fulla selfishness.

**Harold:** Chrissy, I dunno. I done it a million times and come back. Where would I go? Oh, it's breakin' my heart all this wonderful learnin' I'm gettin'. I'm gonna plant some flowers and see if they die or grow. I been with a lot of women, can't

85

no more — why leave? I never understood a minute of it anyway. I remember a little blond girl foamin' at the mouth and yellin' the way she loved me so. But what I thought was goin' on wasn't goin' on. I look at you, Chrissy, I see your skeleton. It's all just shrimp shells and tubing and that's what was going on. Shrimp shells and tubing. I been a fool a lot of years, rollin' around on beds with women thinkin' it was me they loved and them outa everybody, I found 'em at last, when it was just a lot of changes in our blood and stuff and we could leave each other when it was over as easy as we could leave our sweat. They was screamin', beggin' sometimes when I left 'em. It used to make me feel so sad. Women have made me lead a foolish life.

**Chrissy:** Because she was no good for you, you done all that — her never givin' you no children — all them abortions over and over.

**Harold:** Couldn't get no life in her was her problem. She never had none a them done on her. She just used to say that to make me feel bad.

**Chrissy:** What?

**Harold:** Had a wall a meanness up in her, Chrissy. I banged away tryin' ever to break open that meanness. You're the only time I ever got through is how come I love you so. You gimme my life or I wouldn't have any. All that time with women, you're all I got.

**Chrissy:** You never had a good wife is why.

**Harold** (holding up a tomato plant): This here's a tomato plant. Ain't it a beauty?

86

**Chrissy:** You know that's why. If you'da had a good wife, things woulda been different.

**Harold:** Never wanted one is why, Chrissy. Gonna plant this here plant. Water it. Make sure it gets sun an' shade. It'll grow. I'll eat it then. Givin' somethin' life gives you that right, don't you think? It'll be interesting. *(And then, hearing* **Helen** *singing "Hey Daddy, da da da dum . . ." he tenses, looks.)* She's been shopping at the store. *(He yells as* **Helen** *enters.)* You been shopping at the store?

**Helen:** Yes, I have. Two bags full. *(And she carries two shopping bags which she perhaps pantomimes emptying, then slips the empty bags away through the backdrop.)*

**Harold:** Chrissy and me been talkin'.

**Helen:** I was by her apartment.

**Harold** *(shifty-eyed, shuffling, wary):* She wasn't home. I'm gonna go hoe. *(And he turns, grabbing up his plant and tools.)*

**Helen:** I'm gonna be makin' some Kool Aid in a minute if you get thirsty, hon! *(Then, she turns to* **Chrissy***.)* You been over here talkin' to your father.

**Harold** *(yelling from off):* YES, SHE HAS!

**Chrissy:** What of it? *(Carrying her dance bag, perhaps with the coffee thermos in it now, she moves nearer her mother.)*

**Helen:** How was he?

**Chrissy:** Fine.

**Helen:** Don't they play so many nice songs on the radio now-adays? I peeked in the window of your apartment, you know, bringing you oranges. You looked so worried, Chrissy. Are you in the right line of work every person must ask herself. Every person must. Is it your new line of work you're so worried about? I bet you diet and diet.

**Chrissy:** I'm overweight. Don't like it.

**Helen:** To look pretty for your father. He always liked a pretty figure. Except it's a silly business how you gotta wanna have a nice little figure so a man'll wanna get you pregnant and ruin your nice little figure. How tall are you?

**Chrissy:** Why?

**Helen:** Oh, forgive me, honey, I don't mean to pry. It's just I been so nervous and short-tempered lately and so worried about your father. There are moments, I tell you, when I see him sittin' off somewhere lookin' at a wall, or out scratchin' in that dirt, I wish he would want to steal again. The way he used to. He loved to steal things. Made big elaborate plans for big jobs he was goin' to pull someday. Start his own gang.

**Chrissy** (*advancing on her*): Don't you know he's thinking about leavin' you is what he's thinkin' about?

**Helen:** Chrissy, no, no; he's so tired. Home to stay this time. And that's a fact. We gotta be gettin' ready for our little old age. Savin' our money. Doin' our little jobs. Wanna come inside? I'm gonna make him chocolate pudding.

**Chrissy:** But he hates you. I mean, that's what we were talkin' about — how you was a hateful liar. I mean, you never even had any a those abortions I been so worried about.

**Helen:** Do you think about that a lot?

**Chrissy:** I been known to.

**Helen:** And he told you it didn't happen. He never did wanna think about it. Still don't. He's a squeamish man in a lotta ways, but honest to God, Chrissy, he had women sittin' down with coat hangers all across this state. Toilets flushin'; stomachs goin' empty. He just don't bear to think about it — always lovin' little children so. Just never understood the connection. Wanna come in the kitchen? *(She is walking away.)* It's nice inside. Gonna make some chocolate pudding.

**Chrissy:** Are you sayin' you done it?

**Helen:** I always meant to clarify that, Chrissy.

**Chrissy:** Well, I am here to tell you how I am never gonna forgive you — not ever, for how you didn't wanna have me.

**Helen:** Then how come I did? I loved him. How are you to know I loved him? He would lift a can of beer or I would see him standing deep in thought, I would feel such a hurt of love. But I could never make him do what I wanted — be careful — use a thing. "Man don't wear galoshes to take a shower," he would say. So, "I'm pregnant," I would tell him and he would nod and say, "That's good," and pretty soon I would feel him lookin' at my lumpy body, and in his lookin' at me his leavin' of me was clear. I couldn't bear it. So I would get rid of whatever was inside me. I would get rid of it. Except for you. I wanted you.

**Chrissy:** I don't feel good — like my head is shaking; all vibrating. *(She is going sideways a step or two, her knees weak; she looks for a place to rest.)*

**Helen:** I mean, sometimes I forget all 'bout that other stuff. I swear I do, honey.

**Chrissy:** I feel like maybe I can hear what you're thinkin' and I been able maybe all my life. How you hate me. You are in the room with me, I hear you. Outside my door, you stand hatin' me — this goddamn E.S.P. a hate, you —

**Helen:** No, no.

**Chrissy:** Sendin' rays a hate in at me — I hear your thinkin' how I am hateful, all these rays a hate sent in at me into my head! *(And she falls to her knees.)* SHUT UP, SHUT UP! You ain't tellin' me any more. You are done tellin' me. You tried to get rid of me, and you ain't changin' it now. You used to sit on the floor and bounce up and down tryin' to get me out like a hunk a ole blood in that belly and so that's how you always looked at me and me at myself, like I was a little bit dead or that oughta be dead, which is how I regard and look at myself a lot. But I never understood it before. So I wanna get beyond it. I mean, Christ almighty, sometimes I think about what it musta been to be me inside you bouncin' up and down and I wasn't ready to come out. I would only die if I did. How did I feel? How did I feel?

**Helen:** It wasn't you, Chrissy; that wasn't you. No, no.

**Chrissy** *(begging):* Who, then?

**Helen:** I didn't want you dead. Not you.

**Chrissy:** Who?

**Helen:** That thing inside me and all the way it was gonna hurt my life.

**Chrissy:** That was me! *(And she collapses.)*

**Helen:** No! No, I was hesitant in my bouncing. I was hesitant. Something tugged at my heart. I know it did. I coulda bounced harder. I coulda bounced much harder. I coulda jumped off the table. Some tugging at my heart for you held me back or you wouldn't be here. But you are. That's proof of my innermost wishes of hope and love and how they prevailed.

**Chrissy:** Nooo, I don't oughta be dead.

**Helen:** No.

**Chrissy:** Tell me.

**Helen:** You don't oughta be dead. *(And turning, she exits, stepping out of sight through the backdrop.* **Chrissy,** *alone, kneels there. And slowly,* **Chrissy** *stands up, trying to adjust her clothing, picking up her dance bag.)*

**Chrissy:** I gotta stop. I gotta. I 'm gonna stop. *(And turning, she presses the air as if it were a doorbell button. Loudly there is the buzz of a doorbell and the lights go bright and sunny: afternoon. And* **Eric** *comes hastening toward her, hobbling, his leg in a huge thigh-length white cast. He uses a cane.)*

**Eric** *(calling):* Come in! Come in! *(The door buzzer goes again, as he pantomimes opening a door, and there is* **Chrissy.***)* I knew you'd come back. I knew you'd have to come back.

**Chrissy:** Sure.

**Eric:** After that fantastic time at the hotel, I never doubted.

**Chrissy:** I was inna neighborhood, you know.

**Eric:** I haven't been waiting, but it's like I've been waiting.

**Chrissy:** I need help with my astrology, Eric. *(As she digs a book and some papers from her bag.)*

**Eric:** Just last week I drove through the suburbs along the Main Line roads, looking at the houses for sale. I'm very happy with everything.

**Chrissy:** Great. See, I thought you could maybe explain certain things in these astrology books for me. You could help.

**Eric:** I'd be glad to.

**Chrissy:** It's real hard to know some of it.

**Eric** *(as she sits and he settles down next to her, trying to nuzzle her, kiss her):* What was your life like before, Chrissy? I have so very little information on you — I mean, about your life before and away from me. And I feel that if we are to be truly close, we must share everything.

**Chrissy:** Sure. But I mean, what's to know?

**Eric:** Like in that poem I wrote you.

**Chrissy:** That made me feel funny — you callin' me a poem in your poem. I ain't no poem.

**Eric:** I just feel the time has come when I must know more about you.

**Chrissy:** I mean, Eric, WHAT'S TO KNOW?

**Eric:** You see I have been thinking it's time I move downtown.

**Chrissy:** Oh?

**Eric:** Yes. I felt always a deep confidence you would return. Even when my accident immobilized me, I wasn't overly concerned. I knew you would reappear, just as you first appeared. And now you have.

**Chrissy** *(pulling away a little):* Eric, may I ask — downtown where?

**Eric:** You know.

**Chrissy:** No, I don't.

**Eric:** I bet you can guess if you try.

**Chrissy:** I don't wanna guess, but I will 'cause it seems important I should know. My place, right?

**Eric:** But isn't that why you're here?

**Chrissy:** Well, yes and no, Eric. Yes and no. *(Indicating her book, the papers.)* You see, I got all these books and mostly on astrology, and I was wondering if you would help me, as in this one there's about your handwriting.

**Eric:** I already told you I'd be glad to do that.

**Chrissy:** Okay. *(Rapidly, she is paging through the book. She sticks a piece of paper into his hand.)* So here's my handwriting example I brought you, and in the book is what a Libra's handwriting oughta be. You see I'm worried I'm not a Libra. Then I'm guidin' myself to be somethin' I can't ever be it, see?

**Eric:** We wouldn't want that.

**Chrissy:** That's what I'm sayin'. That'd be a mess. So I'll be reading the description of my handwriting, you're lookin' at the sample. *(Eric is gazing at her, wistful and bemused, perhaps he tries to kiss her cheek.)* I mean, you gotta be lookin' at my handwriting example. I gotta see if it fits or not.

**Eric:** I think this is all just a childish evasion of my question.

**Chrissy** *(trying to make him look at the paper):* It ain't a evasion of anything; it's why I come over.

**Eric:** But don't you know, I must know exactly when we can be together permanently, so I can complete my schedule.

**Chrissy:** Eric, listen to me. I mean, I got a goddamn sun, moon and ascendant signs, which I have had since I was born, though I didn't know it. And the planets way up high in the sky have been thinkin' about me and what I should do all my life and this I knew not ever. Then there's this underplace and stuff in there been pushin' at me, too. So we got this stuff way up high like sending down rays at us, and we got this stuff way down deep like sending rays up at us, we don't know anything about any of it. I mean, I'm wondering if maybe all my life the planets been pushing the stuff in my underside. I got maybe my id under Jupiter — my superego thing under the influence of Mars. You understand what I'm sayin' to you, Eric?

**Eric:** Of course I do. You know the feeling I have for you. I love you.

**Chrissy:** Then help me with my goddamn astrology.

**Eric:** I was so glad when they left; I was so glad. Him and that ridiculous Ralphie!

**Chrissy:** Whata you talkin' about?

**Eric:** He was never any good for you, Chrissy. The two of 'em — they were ridiculous. That Ralphie — what was he? What in God's name was he?

**Chrissy:** Whata you been doin'? *(Startled, she stands up.)* I never tole you about no Ralphie. You been followin' me around?

**Eric:** No, no, no.

**Chrissy:** How did you hurt your leg?

**Eric:** It was a stupid accident.

**Chrissy:** How?

**Eric:** It was clumsy of me.

**Chrissy:** The other day there was all this crashin' and bangin' inna alley outside my window, people yellin' some person had fell outa a tree!

**Eric:** No, no, no.

**Chrissy:** Are you a goddamn creep in certain ways? *(And she starts packing to leave.)*

**Eric:** No, no, no. What are you doing? Don't think of leaving.

**Chrissy:** This ain't workin'.

**Eric:** It's working. It's working. Listen to me. I know what you need. Someone has got to look out for you. I have a one-fifty-seven I.Q. I make nearly forty-seven thousand dollars a year.

**Chrissy:** I don't know what you are. You're not a man, Eric. I don't know what you are. I mean, I ain't sayin' you're a queer — I ain't sayin' you're gay, but you make me wanna blink my eyes. I look at you and in my heart I wanna blink my eyes.

**Eric:** Don't you know what I'm offering? A home. Trees. Someone to take care of you.

**Chrissy:** You know, I feel like my thoughts are getting louder. I feel like my thoughts are getting louder and louder.

**Eric:** I want to help you in the fulfillment of your dreams of ballet and other dancing-so-you-tell-a-story of which go-go is just a poor facsimile.

**Chrissy:** Shut up. Are you nuts?

**Eric:** What do you want from me? I don't know what you want. I'll be what you want — tougher — crueler —

**Chrissy:** It don't work that way.

**Eric:** What way does it work, Chrissy? What way does it work?

**Chrissy:** Shut up, Eric! Don't you know you are messing with the universe, Eric! Goddamnit! *(And she is roaring at him, driving him backward toward the edge of the stage.)* I am supposed to be having a very good day and it isn't happening. The

96

stars and planets are getting very angry with you, Eric, so shut up, just shut up. *(Whirling, she marches toward one of the downstage doors.)*

**Eric** *(continuing to back away off and out of sight as the onstage lights are dimming):* When you want me back, I'll be willing. Don't worry. Just call. Just call. *(At the door,* **Chrissy** *knocks, and backs up a few steps, waiting. The door opens and* **Susan** *peeks out, then steps out. It is dark, late night.* **Susan** *is bleary-eyed and dressed in a filmy robe over black panties and bra. She weaves a little on her feet.)*

**Susan:** Jesus, Chrissy, you picked a awful time to come over. Wow, it's late.

**Chrissy:** I know, I know, it's late. I'm sorry. I hadda, though—

**Susan:** I'm busy, see; got company.

**Chrissy:** But . . . I . . . was comin' to see you maybe about us. I wanted a talk. You're maybe right; I don't know. You are the best friend I ever had. I could stay the night . . . maybe.

**A Man** *(his voice coming loudly from offstage):* Who 'zat out there?

**Chrissy** *(startled):* It's a man. You got a man in there? *(Backing away.)*

**Susan:** It's okay. We was just foolin' around a little, we fell asleep. He's a funny guy. We was writin' a song, workin' on writin' a song with music and lyrics. A good one. All about bein' happy. We was working real hard, we fell asleep.

**Chrissy:** I come to see you . . . maybe, Susan. I been thinkin' about what you said.

**Susan:** I know, I know. He'll be gone in the morning. *(And then she laughs, strangely, loudly.)* He's like fuckin' a pony, Chrissy; like fuckin' a pony. I learned some good stuff.

**Chrissy:** Whatsamatter with you? What the hell's a matter with you? Don't you know you are crossing up the stars! You are not a perfect Leo like I thought. *(She has shoved at Susan; she is backing away from Susan.)* You are screwing with the universe, Susan! *(Loudly, a phone rings and Chrissy looks about.)* Don't tell 'em I'm here.

**Susan:** What?

**Chrissy:** Whoever it is, don't tell 'em I'm here.

**Susan** *(drifting back into her own apartment, a little confused, a little angry, and closing the door behind her):* Who's gonna call you here, for crissake?

**Chrissy** *(following Susan, ending up facing the door that has been closed in her face):* I'm tellin' you, I don't know, but I don't want anybody to know about me how I'm here. *(And then she turns and wearily leans against the door, facing out, and slowly speaks.)* I bet it's a pretty song—I bet it's a pretty song you're writin' all about love and screwin'. It's all of 'em sweet songs about it, always, huh, 'cause there ain't nothin' sweet in it, but we gotta do it so much, we gotta think it's sweet. Or see what we are.

*(Music comes on, and Harold and Helen dance on above Chrissy on the upper platforms. The music is bouncy and sentimental and they dance, having fun, whirling and prancing*

98

*as* **Chrissy** *turns to stare up at them, and slowly crosses up to where they are.)*

**Chrissy:** Listen to me, Pops, I'm having a difficult time with a lot of things there's just no point in having a difficult time with 'em. So I gotta talk to you. It's been suggested to me. You got a minute?

**Harold:** I'm a happy man. *(He and* **Helen** *dance on.)*

**Chrissy:** We can discuss some things seriously and quietly.

**Harold:** What about your mother?

**Helen:** It's my house.

**Harold:** Go to another room. You'll still be in your house.

**Chrissy:** I gotta talk.

**Helen:** No, no, I'll close my ears.

**Chrissy:** I wanna know was you in my apartment inna night yesterday, either one a you?

**Helen:** I was here.

**Chrissy:** I come home on my break — an unexpected hour for anybody who knows my schedule. I had a premonition and then I had the feeling someone had been there and they had rushed out when they had a premonition I was coming. Certain things were in different places.

**Helen** *(as she, spinning out of the dance, steps up to* **Chrissy***):* What things?

**Chrissy:** Certain things. A book.

**Helen:** We were up very late last night. Late into the night, talking on and on, together discussing the lovely old times of our youth. In our little old car called Sarah-Silly with a nickel's worth of ice cream — how we'd sit at the bus depot and watch the buses come and go. Waiting for Aunt Milly, we said, our long-lost aunt. *(As the music softens, a new song coming on, a ballad,* **Harold** *and* **Helen** *move into an embrace to dance cheek to cheek.)*

**Chrissy:** I want to know what was our financial status when I was born?

**Helen:** We were very poor. *(They dance.)*

**Harold:** I don't think that's exactly too proper for you to ask.

**Chrissy** *(trying subtly yet desperately to break in on them):* But I want to know. I want to know our exact financial status before and after — how much did we have in the bank?

**Helen:** We had no financial status.

**Harold:** I lived on licorice. Two sticks a day. I looked for work. I lived on licorice and looked for work. Is that what you came here to talk about?

**Chrissy:** No. In a way. Did Aunt Milly ever come?

**Helen:** No.

**Harold:** There was no Aunt Milly.

**Helen:** It was a game we played.

**Chrissy:** And I came.

**Harold:** What? *(They dance on.)*

**Chrissy:** It was a game you played and I came. You waited for Aunt Milly and I came. I came. *(She cannot get their attention.)*

**Harold:** That's a very peculiar thing to say.

**Chrissy:** I've been trying to be orderly.

**Helen:** Good.

**Chrissy** *(somewhat to herself yet to them every once in a while as they dance on, fixed on one another):* I should be orderly, shouldn't I be orderly? I got up very early. I hung up all my clothes. Clothing was all over. I put all the dirty in the hamper, and hung up the clean. Things had been getting out of hand — I hadn't been trying to keep up. You gotta keep up. Everything's moving. Little bitty pieces of stuff, moving and moving. You gotta keep up. How come I can't? I wanna; I wanna. Inna mail, I got back my checks from the bank. I wrote "Banking Material," in big letters. I got all my checks; I put them in order. Then I saw my light bill on the bureau, the gas bill was in by the toilet, all wrinkled, I'd thrown it. *(Gradually, as she speaks, she is moving nearer her father, yet she refers occasionally to her mother.)* But I had no more envelopes. Now I was catching up. There was a drugstore one block toward Center City. And I ran and there were eighty-seven stairs. I had three dirty cups and dishes and a frying pan fulla grease. I did them with Tide. I scrubbed them with Brillo. I vacuumed the front room, I brushed my teeth. I scrubbed the toilet. I washed the windows. I scrubbed my face. I washed my hair. I yelled in the tub. Don't you have anything to tell

101

me? Don't you have anything to tell me? Things have been happening to me, and the other night I was so very drunk, I don't know what happened to me, but something happened and it was either a dream or my real life. I got a phone call. I was sleeping. I woke up and there was this voice asking me about Uncles Billy and Michael and I couldn't tell if it was a man or a woman talking, and then I knew I hadda hang up or the next time I changed my clothes, I wouldn't know if I was a man or a woman. *(And then she screeches to her father, her arm gesturing at her mother.)* Get her outa here! *(Now they have stopped dancing; they move to her.)*

**Helen:** I'm so sorry to see you so upset.

**Chrissy:** Get her outa here!

**Harold** *(leaning toward her, a bottle of whiskey in his hand):* Maybe you could have a little drink?

**Chrissy:** I think somethin' bad was done to me when I was little. I think you did something to me when I was little.

**Harold:** What?

**Chrissy:** Was somethin' bad done to me when I was little? Did you ever do somethin' to me when I was little?

**Harold:** No. Nothing.

**Helen:** I don't know what you mean.

**Chrissy:** I'm tryin' to say for you.

**Harold:** Little thing happened; little, ordinary. We made you eat all your vegetables when we had 'em.

102

**Helen:** What is it that you mean? Is that what you mean?

**Chrissy:** Oh, Christ.

**Harold:** You got no allowance till you were sixteen, and then only a little.

**Chrissy:** Some other person; some other person.

**Harold:** Who?

*(Silence.* **Chrissy** *stares up at him. Something flickers in her eyes. Slowly, she turns, crawls to kneel beside her mother and begins quietly, fearfully, to speak.)*

**Chrissy:** This man very far above me, his big whispering voice, and I kept tryin' to tell him to stop, but I was only crying, 'cause I was a baby. And he . . . was . . . a man! Uncles Billy or Michael when they lived with us. A man. Only I don't know if it happened or if I made it up outa my head. "It's a funny kinda finger," he said. "Just a funny kinda finger. Don't tell anybody." "You touched me," I said. Only I was crying. Only I don't know if it happened or if it didn't.

*(Pause.)*

**Helen:** No.

**Harold:** I would say not. No.

*(***Chrissy** *turns away from her mother; she turns to her father.)*

**Helen:** No. I would say not.

**Harold:** No.

**Chrissy:** Poppa, Momma, please! If I hear these voices in my head sayin' it's you and you love me, I should do what you want, who is it?

*(Pause.)*

**Helen:** You.

**Harold:** You, honey.

**Helen:** Nobody's in your head but you. You're in your own head.

**Harold:** We're each in his own head.

**Helen:** You're in your head. Your poppa's in his head.

**Harold:** I'm in my head.

**Helen:** Your poppa's in his head. We're each in his own head. All that's just something you always wanted, but not a soul ever did it to you. I always knew that about you.

**Chrissy:** What?

**Helen:** It never happened, Chrissy. We'd have heard.

**Harold:** Of course we would have; we'd have known.

**Chrissy** *(her voice a little infantile):* I was worried.

**Helen:** Of course you were.

**Chrissy** *(still childlike):* I hadda try and find out.

**Helen:** Of course you did.

**Chrissy:** I came over to find out if it happened; and now I'm going home after finding out it didn't. *(And she has begun a long journey to leave.)*

**Helen:** That's right.

**Harold:** Don't you want any supper?

**Helen:** She's not hungry, Harry. Are you, hon?

**Chrissy:** No.

**Helen:** See?

**Chrissy:** I gotta go cook my own dinner.

**Helen:** She's gotta go cook dinner for her own man. The way to a man's heart is through his stomach, Chrissy.

**Chrissy:** The way to a man's heart is through his stomach.

*(They have pivoted now so **Chrissy**, while waving "Bye-bye" to them, is backing downstage, as **Harold** and **Helen** pivot and face out while moving deeper and deeper upstage.)*

**Helen:** That's right.

**Harold:** Bye-bye.

**Chrissy:** Bye-bye.

**Helen:** Bye-bye.

**Harold:** Bye-bye.

**Chrissy:** Bye-bye.

*(At the far downstage corner,* **Chrissy** *encounters* **Al** *who has entered in the dark and now sits, his battered suitcase beside him.)*

**Helen:** Bye-bye.

*(***Al** *and* **Chrissy** *see each other,* **Chrissy** *reaching toward him.)*

**Al:** Got back into town, come by first thing.

**Chrissy:** How was your trip?

**Al:** Been inna hospital. Stupid disease. Drinkin' disease in my body. Educational inna hospital, however, very educational. Many things to be learned for he of the alert ear and eye. The "O" and the "Q" and the "corn flakes position" are mostly unknown, I would say. Would you say? *(Moving nearer to her, he is bragging.)* I eavesdropped, and learned a number of things, for example, the little secret names the doctors give among themselves to the ways people die. "O" is with your mouth open. And "Q" is with your mouth open and your tongue sticking out. And the "corn flake position" is when they find the patient dead with his face in the breakfast food. You ever hear a any a that? I come to you right away to tell you, I want the "O." And my mouth closed and you on one side, your mom and dad on the other, our children all around. We'll all hold hands.

**Chrissy:** You don't have any children.

**Al:** I'm askin' you. Arrange it. Have I ever denied you anything?

106

**Chrissy:** Yes.

**Al:** Don't hold it against me.

**Chrissy:** What are you sayin' to me?

**Al:** You can arrange it. Do some big deals. Lie! I been known to recently answer phones that ain't even ringin'. I had a hell of a week — Ralphie got run over by a truck. Run him right over, breakin' all his arms and legs, him screamin' it was my fault, and it wasn't. Sometimes they grab the phone away from me. "It didn't ring," they yell. I wait; I pick it back up. "Hello," I say. Now get those children; arrange it; get that family. Even niggers got families. *(And suddenly, in the last sentence, he is begging.)*

**Chrissy:** Oh, Al. Wanna go upstairs? I'll take you upstairs. Have some coffee. Some soup. I'll cook some soup for you, Al.

**Al:** I'll wait'll it's there, before I eat it. *(As* **Chrissy** *and* **Al** *leave,* **Harold** *and* **Helen** *are revealed in light upstage where they were, staring out, sitting.)*

**Helen:** Look at you.

**Harold:** I'm a good example.

**Helen:** Look at you.

**Harold:** There's no point in talkin' odd, Helen. There's jokes all over the world.

**Helen:** What was you thinkin'?

**Harold:** I am listenin' to you very closely, Helen.

**Helen:** Didn't you always call it your funny finger? Your funny finger between your legs.

**Harold:** As you know, I have been having problems in my memory since my illness onset.

**Helen:** But wouldn't *I* remember?

**Harold:** I may have and I may not have.

**Helen** *(mocking him):* You may have and you may not have.

**Harold:** Did I not call many things my funny finger after callin' it my funny finger? Many and various things, if you may remember. A broom, did I not? Or my thumb, I would tickle her belly, or your belly: "It's a-comin'; it's a-comin'." Or a broom — I would run around the yard at night wavin' it, callin' it my giant funny finger. If you may remember. Or a baseball bat. Did I not do all that? Do you not remember?

**Helen:** What was you thinkin'?

**Harold:** When?

**Helen:** When you did it?

**Harold:** And even if you do not remember, your evidence is only hearsay which is inadmissible, and even if it is, only circumstantial.

**Helen:** This is not a court of law. This is a home. This is a family.

**Harold:** I agree with you! Oh, I am lonely. I miss them. I did all I could, but I could not keep up. There were too many.

You see them and see them every spring and summer. Bare brown bellies, waiting to be filled, like flowers. There's such a gorgeousness in 'em — such a gorgeousness in all the flowers of the world. I wish I was a bee. There wouldn't be too many. I could fly. WHAT A BEE I'D BE! WHAT A FUCKIN' BEE I'D BE. *(He takes a big drink of water.)* She was so small. I would throw her. I would catch her. And I will admit that I thought playfully and lightheartedly of doing something I shouldn't in a playful and lighthearted manner, but I resisted always. Never ever did I do no such thing as she says was done to her. For Uncles Billy and Michael, though, how have I any way of knowing or speaking? They may have found the temptation of her irresistible — it is not impossible — for she was a lovely little woman always AND YOU COULD SEE HOW SHE WANTED IT! Now . . . I . . . asked about the whereabouts of the most recent edition of *Mobster Magazine*. I have been asking and asking.

**Helen:** I know that.

**Harold:** But where is it? I don't see it.

**Helen:** I don't even feel sorry for her.

**Harold:** We are done with our talking on and on about Chrissy and I do not feel sorry for her either. It is for you for whom I feel sorry, for you are so forgetful — forgetting how little I sometimes like to hear your voice. It is one of those times. So I offer advice. Put into working order that portion of your brain that selects what words going round in your head will get to come out your mouth and select **NONE**. Go check in the mailbox for the recent edition of *Mobster*. Tommy Leroy Luckritz said the picture on the cover was a picture of Dutch Schultz of Chicago. I will be on the porch. *(Helen runs off.)* Bring it to me on the porch. Do it now before I begin crying and crying and in my sadness beat the shit out of you.

*(He exits in the opposite direction. Music has begun as he said "NONE." And now, as he goes off and* Chrissy *comes into view, wearing a bright dress, carrying flowers, ribbons in her hair, the music builds. And all the girls but* Susan *join* Chrissy *for her Go-Go Wedding.)*

**Chrissy:** I'm so happy to be gettin' married. I'm so happy to be finally gettin' married. I mean, I have come to understand at last how I have lived my life so far stupid, and people'll never be happy livin' the way I have. I mean, cruel and mean and selfish. When I don't got a self in me . . . even. No . . . real self. But I have other virtues. I am honest, basically, and I know the mistake my mother made, 'cause when she got her man, she did everything she could to break him and crush him, but he was unbreakable. In his spirit. Poppa was unbreakable. And that's not a thing I'll ever do. I'll help my man. I'll be for him, and that way I'll never end up like her. Never end up like Susan. I mean, I think Susan is cruel and without no womanly feelings. She is like my mother. A man in disguise. *(The music is lyrical, full of yearning. Perhaps the girls put a veil on* Chrissy, *a little shawl of lace.)* I don't know how it happens, but a woman is tenderness and love. Just tenderness and love no matter what her body. I don't even know if what I'm talkin' about sometimes ever even really happened, but I am gonna be dedicated to the one I love. We'll be married and regular and I'll be happy havin' a life fixin' the terrible hurt in Al so he's happy.

**Vikki:** You mean you'll have someone to care for.

**Chrissy:** Yes.

**Melissa:** And he'll care for you.

**Sally:** As you are.

**Chrissy:** Yes.

**Sally:** You'll be strong.

**Chrissy:** I'll be strong.

**Melissa:** Love him in some crazy way you don't even understand it.

**Chrissy:** I'm gonna love him in some crazy way I won't even understand it myself. And he'll need me. Be like Martha and the Vandellas doin' "My Baby Needs Me." Aretha and "My Place in the Sun."

**Melissa:** Gonna be for once in a lifetime.

**Sally:** Ain't no mountain high enough.

**Chrissy:** You ain't makin' fun a me! *(Around her now, the girls are dancing as the music swells and moves them.* **Chrissy***, trying to fit into the rhythms, tries still to talk to them.)* You ain't makin' fun a me!

**Melissa:** No, no.

**Chrissy:** It's true.

**Vikki:** We know.

**Chrissy:** It's true.

**Melissa:** We all know.

111

*(As below them,* Al *has entered to stand, rather formally, looking up.)*

Chrissy: It'll be what I dreamed of. I won't care about anything but him. How can I lose it? *(And the girls dance, as* Chrissy *moves toward* Al, *her attention fixed on him.)*

Vikki: You can't!

Sally: You can't! *(And they all dance behind* Chrissy.*)*

Chrissy *(facing* Al*):* It'll be me. Al'll be all that I am. I can't ever lose it! I won't ever lose it. *(Turning, she throws her bouquet of flowers up to the girls, one of whom catches it, and then* Chrissy *leaps into* Al's *arms.)* Gonna be happy together, 'cause my baby needs me. Gonna be forever my love — everything so good about him. *(Hand in hand,* Chrissy *and* Al *run off.)*

Melissa: Gonna be happy together, 'cause my baby needs me. Gonna be forever my love.

Vikki: I'm so happy for you.

Melissa: Everything so good about him! *(The girls dance, waving farewell.)*

Vikki: I'm so happy for you, Chrissy.

Sally: I'm so happy for you! *(The lights are dimming on the girls as they wave farewell and drift upstage.)*

Melissa: I'm so happy for you.

Vikki: I'm so happy for you! *(As* Chrissy *enters from the bath-*

*room door of her apartment. She wears a tattered old blue robe.)*

**Melissa:** So happy for you, so happy for you.

*(Harsh, funky music comes on loudly now, an angry tone and beat as the lights come up on* **Chrissy's** *apartment and go out on the girls, who exit, slipping through the backdrop.* **Chrissy** *paces angrily as the music pounds away. The light is bright but harsh, bare. The music pounds.* **Chrissy** *paces.* **Al** *enters; he wears dirty work clothes. He and* **Chrissy** *stand a second, staring at each other; then* **Al** *walks to the bed and turns a switch, turning off the radio. The music cuts out. Silence.)*

**Chrissy:** How come you didn't call me?

**Al:** I called you.

**Chrissy:** I sat around waitin', for crissake.

**Al:** I got a recordin'. I kept callin' and gettin' this recorded bitch tellin' me the phone was outa order.

**Chrissy:** It ain't outa order.

**Al:** I know it ain't.

**Chrissy:** It's you who's the one who's outa order. And how come you gotta be callin' her a bitch anyway? You don't know her.

**Al:** Don't mess with me.

**Chrissy:** How come you gotta be callin' everybody names alla time? I said, how come you gotta call her a bitch?

113

**Al:** 'Cause that's what she was. They get that tone a voice first day on the job. Cunty. Like their shit don't stink. I seen a lot of 'em.

**Chrissy:** That's all women are to you, ain't it?

**Al:** Don't you start on me, Chrissy!

**Chrissy:** Am I startin' on you?

**Al:** It feels like it.

**Chrissy:** It feels like I'm startin' on you, does it? I mean, I don't even know how come I gotta be puttin' up with you.

**Al:** Anytime you want; anytime you want!

**Chrissy:** I mean, you are such a deep-feeling person. You got so many deep feelings!

**Al:** Awwww, fuck you. *(And he flops back down in the chair.)*

**Chrissy:** I wish you would. *(She joins him.)*

**Al:** I hadda lotta things go wrong today; you gimme a break, I'm warnin' you, goddamnit.

**Chrissy:** What kinda thing are you to warn me? What kinda thing are you to have around, even? I got needs, see. Al Royce. *(She reaches inside his shirt to rub his chest.)* Big Al Royce. What's that? I ain't just a hunk of liver for you to pound on!

**Al:** Oh, my Christ, I really gotta deal with you, don't I?

**Chrissy** *(moving to unbuckle his belt)*: Am I sayin' you don't?

I'm ...... ..... (w) ..'kin', see. And it's me who
do.... .................. .ullshit for a change, see.
I ........................ ..lt days lately, some very
tr.................... ..etimes how my thoughts
a............... ...d everybody can hear 'em,
j......... ...t.

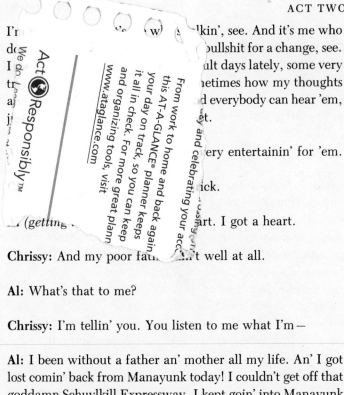

................ ...y and celebrating your acc... ...ery entertainin' for 'em.

.......... ...ick.

... (getting .......art. I got a heart.

**Chrissy:** And my poor fat.... ...'t well at all.

**Al:** What's that to me?

**Chrissy:** I'm tellin' you. You listen to me what I'm —

**Al:** I been without a father an' mother all my life. An' I got lost comin' back from Manayunk today! I couldn't get off that goddamn Schuylkill Expressway. I kept goin' into Manayunk and back on that Roosevelt Boulevard. I COULDN'T GET IN THE RIGHT FUCKIN' LANE!

**Chrissy:** I don't care about that!

**Al:** You woulda if you was with me!

**Chrissy:** You shoulda called!

**Al:** I tried.

**Chrissy** *(rushing after him):* That ain't what we're talkin' about anyway. We're talkin' about me and the fact that I gotta

115

assert myself. You don't assert yourself and people shit all over you. I don't wanna be hard, but if that's how you gotta be, I'm gonna do it. Gonna be a hammer and everybody else is nails in a world of wood! Are you hearin' me? You listen to me what I'm sayin' for I am very uptight for I am extremely nervous a lot 'cause I am worried over my life.

**Al:** You got every right to be.

**Chrissy:** Listen to me what I'm sayin'! On a subway today, I was sitting there and I was thinkin' so hard I was lost in thought — I was lost in it — and then all of a sudden I saw I was doin' funny things with my hands, making funny signs in the air with my hands and this person next to me was lookin' at me and I looked at them, sittin' there, and I just says, "I'm goin' crazy." It just come outa me like I was sayin' it was rainin' — "I'm goin' crazy" and she didn't say "No." She didn't. She just looks away and moves real quick a couple seats down the aisle. *(She moves at him now, attacking, cornering him back on the bed.)* So I wanna relax, Big Al, I want you to pour me a drink. I want you to give me a rubdown. I want you to ball me real good for a change — if you could manage that — so I get off — so I get off good for a change insteada givin' you blow jobs all the time, which I don't mind for variety, but as a steady diet, it brings to mind the lyrics from that old and much loved song — "I knew this dance was gonna be a drag," and which — by the way — you could get a whole lot readier and no doubt better off some faggot if that is your need. AM I MAKIN' MYSELF CLEAR, BIG AL? *(She is all but ripping his clothes off him, and he pulls away, shoving her off, as he paces away.)*

**Al:** I mean, ain't it somethin'? So I spend the day in that god-damn truck gettin' my kidneys bounced around in my ribs like they're fuckin' pool balls, so I finally get home and there's this

116

girl here in my house at that time a the month when she's in full flush a her lesbian tendencies!

**Chrissy** (*staring for an instant*): Oh, my God!

**Al:** You ever think that? You ever think you got maybe lesbian tendencies? You ever think that, huh?

**Chrissy:** No.

**Al:** No? No?

**Chrissy:** "NO," I THINK IS WHAT I SAID.

**Al:** Then how come it took you so long to say it? How come there was that silence?

**Chrissy:** I know people who got 'em.

**Al:** Is that right? You know people who got 'em.

**Chrissy:** How come you gotta repeat everything I say?

**Al:** Because most of the stuff you say is so fuckin' unbelievable I gotta hear it twice before I can believe anybody in this world could be so stupid as to say it once, let alone twice!

**Chrissy:** I know people who got 'em.

**Al:** Is that right?

**Chrissy:** Yeh. I travel and work in widely mixtured company, as you might know, and sometimes the girls got 'em.

**Al:** The girls at work, you're sayin'. So then how does that explain certain events I know of? How does that explain the way I saw you lookin' at the train station, for example?

**Chrissy** (*not knowing what he's talking about*): What train station?

**Al:** We was together.

**Chrissy:** What train station?

**Al:** You know.

**Chrissy** (*still unsure*): We been together in a lot of train stations.

**Al:** Big girl. Blonde.

**Chrissy:** I was lookin' at her clothes.

**Al** (*very cocky, very sarcastic; striding about*): I mean, she had on that kinda hat and that kinda jacket and that kinda shoes. Very special. Oh, yah; you just gave her the old up-down look, startin' at her toes and goin' right on up. Right on up.

**Chrissy** (*as far as she is concerned, it is ridiculous for him to bring up that she looked at a woman*): I seen you lookin' at men sometimes.

**Al:** Don't try and turn it around. I'm too smart for that.

**Chrissy:** I seen it.

**Al** (*like a child, so happy he's nearly jumping up and down*): You're gropin'; I hit you where it hurts.

118

**Chrissy:** I seen you lookin' at niggers.

**Al:** Don't talk to me about niggers.

**Chrissy** *(very confused):* And anyway, I was lookin' at her clothes.

**Al:** I don't take no shit off niggers!

**Chrissy:** She was wearin' this beautiful pants suit the color a sandalwood!

**Al:** Is that right?

**Chrissy** *(just trying to straighten it all out):* I'm tellin' you.

**Al:** The only look I look at niggers with is how I want to kill 'em!

**Chrissy:** I was lookin' at her clothes!

**Al:** How come you are talkin' to me about niggers?

**Chrissy:** What're you askin' me?

**Al:** I'm askin' you how come you're talkin' to me about niggers!

**Chrissy** *(defensively):* I got my reasons.

**Al:** I don't wanna know 'em. I don't wanna know nothin' about you and niggers. You been with 'em; I know you have.

**Chrissy** *(thinking that's ridiculous):* No, I ain't.

119

**Al:** Bullshit!

**Chrissy:** No, I ain't. I'm tellin' you, I ain't!

**Al** *(exploding in front of her):* I'll burn you your fuckin' snatch clean you do, you hear me? I'll put a hot poker up you, make you clean, you hear me? I spit at 'em on the street. Niggers ain't shit, man; they ain't nothin'. Two and three of 'em used to beat me up when I was a kid. They used to jump me, take me to knuckle city, but I'd get one of 'em alone it was different. I used to grind 'em up, spit 'em out. Niggers ain't shit, man! One on one they'd be tough for a little, but little by little — kick 'em in the shins — they'd come apart. No endurance. Couldn't last, see: and I think it was because a their nutrition; they wasn't gettin' good food like I was. I mean, they was all poorer than me, even, and two or three of 'em would do a job on me. Then I'd get one of 'em, and I'd clock'm — I'd put out his lights. But now they're gettin' better food or somethin', they're gettin' good nutrition — I mean, you seen the size a some a them spooks. It never used to be that way. It never used to be that way. I mean, they ain't shit; niggers ain't shit. *(It has all rushed out of him like vomit and hysteria, leaving him shaken, nearly exhausted.)*

**Chrissy:** That really makes you squirm, don't it.

**Al:** It don't make me squirm.

**Chrissy:** How come it makes you squirm?

**Al:** It don't.

**Chrissy:** You're squirmin' now.

**Al:** I'm tellin' you it don't make me squirm.

120

**Chrissy:** You ain't tellin' me nothin' no more, Daddyo!

**Al:** About niggers, I am.

**Chrissy:** About nothin'. Susan says if I wanna go out with a black man, I can and I —

**Al:** Don't call 'em that.

**Chrissy:** I'll call 'em what I wanna.

**Al:** Don't call 'em no black man. They ain't no black man. They are niggers! Niggers!

**Chrissy:** I think they got a right to call themselves what they wanna call themselves and that's what they wanna call themselves. It's in all the papers. It's always in the papers.

**Al:** How come I gotta be stuck with you? How come I gotta be stuck with such a stupid goddamn stupid bitch?

**Chrissy:** But I ain't listenin' to you any more, Daddyo! Don't you know how I ain't listenin'? I am a free person — a free goddamn person. Susan says, don't have to ball nobody I don't wanna, cook what anybody wants to eat. I can ball even niggers if I wanna!

**Al:** I'll put you in the toilet you don't shut up — I'll flush you down the goddamn toilet!

**Chrissy:** But I ain't listenin' to you any more, Daddyo!

**Al:** Shut up!

**Chrissy:** You ain't makin' me feel stupid and low and hateful

121

and guilty 'cause you ain't got your freedom — you ain't got your life, when it's you who done it to me, over and over, tryin' to jam me up into her who you hate and leavin' me there for her to get me out like a hunk of ole waste in a belly. You shoulda put me in a woman you loved and I am through with you!

**Al:** I don't know what you're talkin' about!

**Chrissy:** I know what I'm talkin' about. I KNOW WHAT I'M TALKIN' ABOUT!

**Al:** Chrissy, I wanna take a nap — I'm wasted. *(And he flops onto the bed, putting a pillow over his head, but she will not let him alone. She marches to him.)*

**Chrissy:** And I have made up my mind to be ballin' niggers!

**Al:** You know why the lady on the subway nodded in agreement when you tole her on the subway you was goin' crazy, because you very well are!

**Chrissy:** I'll be bringin' them back here, too, Albert.

**Al:** Lemme alone!

**Chrissy:** I'll be bringin' 'em all back right here.

**Al:** No, you won't.

**Chrissy:** I will; I will. I'll report it to you. I'll get 'em to treat me bad!

**Al:** Don't tell me that.

**Chrissy:** It's what I'm gonna do; I'll make you wash the dishes, Albert; I'll make you wash the sheets.

**Al:** I ain't gonna be here. I'm gonna be gone. *(Running, he rams open the bathroom door and leaps in grabbing his suitcase and a pile of clothing.)*

**Chrissy:** No, you ain't gonna be gone.

**Al:** I am, too, gonna be gone.

**Chrissy:** No, you ain't. You are gonna be here. You are gonna see it!

**Al:** Shut the fuck up. I'm tellin' you, I'm gonna be gone. *(He hurls the suitcase onto the floor and begins throwing the clothing into it, as she struggles to pull the clothes out.)* I got nothin' here. Whata I got here? A job I hate and a whore who hates me and's goin' crazy into the bargain. Whata I need with you? I'm goin'. Gettin' on. Miami. Vegas.

**Chrissy:** I'll find you, Albert. I'll find out where you are.

**Al:** Lemme alone.

**Chrissy:** You ain't gonna get away for what you done to me! *(As he moves to the bathroom or a drawer in the bed to get more things, she dumps the suitcase on the floor.)*

**Al:** Shut up!

**Chrissy:** I'll send you movies, Albert. That's what I'll do. I'll send you movies of it. Black-and-white, Albert. Movies. Close-ups. I'll get cameras all around the bed. I'll get it from all

123

directions. (*Now* **Al** *is trying to stuff everything back into the suitcase while she tugs on a piece of clothing, and they are tugging in opposite directions, an idiotic tug of war over the clothing.*) I'll find out where you are. You'll get it inna mail. I'll get some rhythm outa my screwin'! (*Now he pivots and grabs her, screaming, his fist slamming into her stomach.*)

**Al:** You been hurtin' me! (*And she cries out and goes down. He is on top of her, she is crying out.*) You been hurtin' me! You been hurtin' me! (*He is pounding her and she is crying out.*)

**Chrissy:** Ohhhhh!

**Al:** You been hurtin' me!

**Chrissy:** Don't hit my face!

**Al** (*hitting again and again*): You been hurtin' me.

**Chrissy:** Don't hit my face, don't hit my stomach. (*And the lights go dark on them.*) Don't hit my face, don't hit my stomach, don't hit my face, don't hit my stomach. (*Even as* **Chrissy** *is still yelling in the dark, a bright spotlight hits the man who stands in the elevated area, a corner intensely lit by the spot. He wears a dark suit, the collar open, the tie — if he wears one — is loose and there is a drooping flower in his lapel.*)

**The Man:** As you all know if you're regulars, it is our degenerate and abhorrent practice here to let a new little girl upon her arrival here have a little kind of introduction to her fans, and we got a new little girl tonight just up from Philadelphia to go to work in the Big Apple — gonna shine her light in Fun City — and she calls herself the "Masked Rider." (*He pumps his fist in the air, but the gesture has little enthusiasm.*)

"You got your choice," she says when I was talkin' to her. "What's it gonna be, face or boobies?" "Boobies," we told her. "Boobies, boobies, boobies." And as you also know, if you are a regular, it is also our degenerate and abhorrent practice, whoooo whooooo . . . *(pumping his fist halfheartedly in the air)* to let the little filly do her New York bare-boobie debut as a solo to a song of her own selection. What's it gonna be, Masked Rider?

*(**Chrissy** lifts her head and she is wearing a mask. Her eyes can be seen.)*

**Chrissy:** E–seven. *(And the music starts and **Chrissy** is rising to her feet. Her breasts are bare. She wears a small, bikini-like bottom. She stands, waiting. The music is playing.)*

**The Man:** Now, she's been workin' real hard all her life to get this just right. You give her your undivided attention.

*(The music is loud and **Chrissy**, half naked, dances. She dances to the music. Perhaps the music changes or cuts out and still, half-naked on the otherwise empty stage, she dances.)*

BLACKOUT

END OF PLAY

# AUTHOR'S NOTE

This revision is essentially a return to the two-act construction in which the play was originally written and performed at Villanova University in 1972. Between that initial staging and the Lincoln Center presentation the following year, material was added: a scene, some speeches and amplifications of moments, all of which occurred in the first act (of the two-act version), with the result that the first act became excessively long for this format. At the time, however, no adequate strategy for cutting could be determined. The pressures of the moment then effectively prohibited any dispassionate evaluation, and suggestions centered around the elimination of one scene or another, a tactic which was, from my vantage, not possible. Eventually I opted for the makeshift solution of a three-act construction — a forced measure, I knew, a change of pace rather than a real solution; but it was the best I could devise under the circumstances. It was in this form, then, that the play went to publication; and so it has remained until this time, as has my dissatisfaction with it.

Given the recent invitation to republish by Grove Press, I saw, in the coincidental off-Broadway production of the play by the Orange Theatre Company, an opportunity to try once more to resolve the difficulties of the text effectively. What I realized, after some thought and experimentation, was that the organic nature of the play demanded a return to the two-act construction. For best effect, the second-act material had to flow from one event to the next, and the scene and speech which had originally ended the first act were meant to serve

127

that purpose. What I also determined was that the necessary cutting could be managed without the amputation of any single scene in its entirety, but rather through a sequence of minor snips of lines and speeches, which, in their accumulation, would return to the play the original balance which had been thrown off by those first additions.

DAVID RABE